D0507360

Geometry Basics
Grades 5–8

Authors: Schyrlet Cameron and Carolyn Craig
Editor: Mary Dieterich
Proofreaders: April Albert and Margaret Brown

COPYRIGHT © 2016 Mark Twain Media, Inc.

ISBN 978-1-62223-582-7

Printing No. CD-404237

Mark Twain Media, Inc., Publishers
Distributed by Carson-Dellosa Publishing LLC

The purchase of this book entitles the buyer to reproduce the student pages for classroom use only. Other permissions may be obtained by writing Mark Twain Media, Inc., Publishers.

All rights reserved. Printed in the United States of America.

Table of Contents

Introduction to the Teacher

Geometry concepts are an integral part of performing higher math skills. What is learned at one grade level is built upon at the next grade level. Standards for mathematics suggest part of the instructional time for grades five through eight should concentrate on geometry.

Geometry Basics targets the basic concepts needed to build a solid base for understanding and performing operations involving higher math. It focuses on helping students gain strong foundations, including a solid understanding of concepts, a high degree of procedural skill and fluency, and the ability to apply the math they know to solve problems inside and outside the classroom. The structure of the content and presentation of concepts and skills in this book support the State Standards for Mathematics.

The book is divided into five units. The units provide instruction for concepts that are the basis for all geometry: Lines and Angles; Two-Dimensional Figures; Circles; Three-Dimensional Figures; and Perimeter, Area, and Volume. Units are divided into several lessons. Each lesson covers one concept.

Features of the book include:

- **Lesson Introduction** is designed as a teacher-guided introduction of the concepts and skills presented in the lesson. Each page includes the lesson objective, state standards, vocabulary, definitions, overview of skills, concepts to be taught, example problems, sample problems to try with the students, and a real-world connection for the skill.

- **Practice** is a page of exercises involving concepts and skills presented in the Lesson Introduction.

- **Assessment** is an evaluation of what the student has learned in each unit. Each assessment is presented in standardized-test format.

- **Glossary** is an organized list of the domain-specific vocabulary presented in the book.

Geometry Basics offers teachers a wide variety of instructional options to meet the diverse learning styles of middle-school students. The book can be used to introduce, review, or reinforce geometry skills and concepts needed by middle-school students. The lessons can be used for whole-group or small-group instruction, independent practice, or homework. It can be used to supplement or enhance the regular classroom curriculum or with Title I instruction.

Lesson Introduction: Points, Lines, and Rays

State Standards	Objective
• Math.Content.5-8 Geometry	• Identify basic terms and symbols of geometry.

Vocabulary

congruent segments, geometry, intersecting lines, line, line segment, parallel lines, perpendicular lines, point, ray

Overview

Geometry is a branch of mathematics that deals with points, lines, shapes, and space. Points, lines, line segments, and rays are the basic terms of geometry used to describe and define other terms in geometry. Points on a line are named by capital letters.

Common Terms

Term	Example	Symbol
Point: a single location or position (•)	• A	•A point A
Line: a straight path that is endless in both directions (↔)	A B	$\overleftrightarrow{AB}$ or $\overleftrightarrow{BA}$ line AB or line BA
Line Ray: a part of a line that extends in one direction from one endpoint (→)	R S	$\overrightarrow{RS}$ ray RS
Line Segment: a part of a line between two endpoints (___)	G H	$\overline{GH}$ segment GH
Congruent Segments: line segments that have the same lengths (≅)	A B P Q	$\overline{AB} \cong \overline{PQ}$ line AB is congruent to line PQ
Intersecting Lines: lines that meet at a point (∩)	H N M O K	$\overleftrightarrow{NM} \cap \overleftrightarrow{KH}$ line NM intersects line KH
Parallel Lines: lines that never intersect (∥)	A B P Q	$\overleftrightarrow{AB} \parallel \overleftrightarrow{PQ}$ line AB is parallel to line PQ
Perpendicular Lines: lines that intersect to form right angles (⊥)	U S V T	$\overleftrightarrow{ST} \perp \overleftrightarrow{UV}$ line ST is perpendicular to line UV

Problems to Try

1. Name the line.   F   G   **Answer:** $\overleftrightarrow{FG}$ or $\overleftrightarrow{GF}$

2. Name the ray.   U   V   **Answer:** $\overrightarrow{VU}$

Real-World Connection

The natural world is filled with things made up of geometric shapes, such as traffic signs, railroad tracks, and cereal boxes.

Name: _____   Date: _____

Practice: Points, Lines, and Rays

Write *parallel, perpendicular,* or *intersecting* to describe each set of lines.

 1.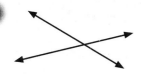

2.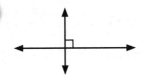

3.

_____   _____   _____

Use the figure below to answer questions 4 through 6. Use the symbols for lines, line segments, and rays in your answer.

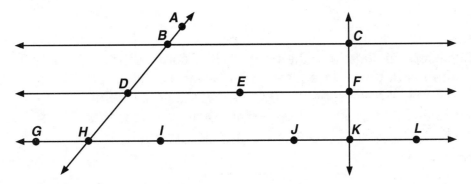

4. Give an example of a line segment. _____

5. Give an example of a line. _____

6. Give an example of a ray. _____

Use the figure below to answer questions 7 through 10. Write *parallel, perpendicular,* or *intersecting* for each pair of lines.

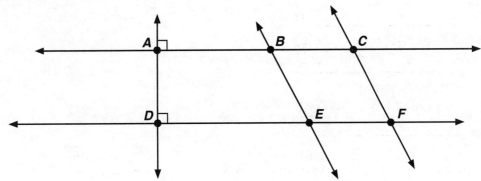

7. $\overleftrightarrow{AC}$ and $\overleftrightarrow{DF}$ _____

9. $\overleftrightarrow{BE}$ and $\overleftrightarrow{CF}$ _____

8. $\overleftrightarrow{BE}$ and $\overleftrightarrow{AC}$ _____

10. $\overleftrightarrow{DF}$ and $\overleftrightarrow{BE}$ _____

Lesson Introduction: Relationships Among Points, Lines, and Planes

State Standards	Objective
• Math.Content.5-8 Geometry	• Analyze relationships among points, lines, and planes.

Vocabulary
collinear points, coplanar lines, non-collinear points, plane, skew lines

Overview
In geometry, definitions are formed using known words or terms to describe a new word. A **plane** is an undefined mathematical term. It has no thickness but extends indefinitely in all directions. The flat surface of a table top suggests a portion of a plane. Imagine that the surface of the table top is extended in all directions. A plane contains an unlimited number of points, segments, line rays, and so on.

This imaginary unlimited flat surface to the right may be considered as a representation of the set of points in a plane. Planes are usually represented by a shape that looks like a parallelogram. Even though the diagram of a plane has edges, remember that a plane has no boundaries. A plane is named by a single letter in a script font (plane m) or by three non-collinear points (plane STR).

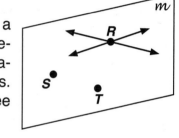

Collinear Points: points that lie on the same straight line

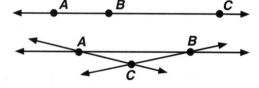

Non-collinear Points: three or more points not in the same straight line

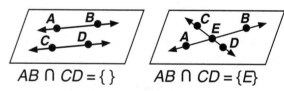

Coplanar Lines: two lines in the same plane. Any two coplanar lines either intersect or are parallel. Two coplanar lines are parallel if their intersection is the empty set ({ }).

$AB \cap CD = \{ \}$ $AB \cap CD = \{E\}$

Skew Lines: straight lines in different planes that do not intersect and are not parallel; ($\overleftrightarrow{XY}$ and $\overleftrightarrow{CD}$ are skew lines.)

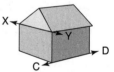

Problem to Try
Which lines are skew?

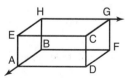

A. $\overleftrightarrow{AB}$ and $\overleftrightarrow{DF}$

B. $\overleftrightarrow{HE}$ and $\overleftrightarrow{GC}$

C. $\overleftrightarrow{HE}$ and $\overleftrightarrow{BA}$

D. $\overleftrightarrow{HG}$ and $\overleftrightarrow{FD}$

Answer: D

Real-World Connection
Many professionals need to understand the properties of shapes, including engineers and architects.

Name: _____   Date: _____

Practice: Relationships Among Points, Lines, and Planes

Write *collinear, non-collinear,* or *coplanar* to describe the lines.

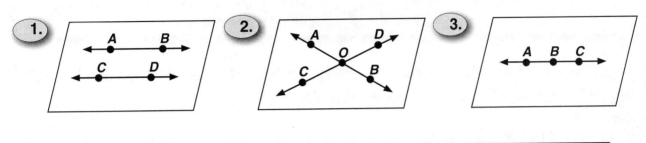

1.   2.   3.

_____   _____   _____

In the exercises below, the dots represent points in a plane. Use a ruler to connect the dots in all possible ways. Predict the number of possible segments by counting the number of points before drawing.

L • M • A	L • N • M • B	L • O • N • M • C
L • P • M • N • O • D	L • Q • M • P • N • O • E	L • R • Q • M • N • O • P • F

Use the pattern you discovered in the above exercises to complete the following table.

Plane	Number of Points	Number of Segments
A	2	1
B	3	3
C	4	6
D	5	10
4. E	6	
5. F	7	
6. 8		
7. 9		
8. 10		

9. What is the relationship between the number of points and the total number of segments?

_____

_____

_____

Let **p** represent the number of points.

Let **s** represent the number of segments.

s = _____

_____

Lesson Introduction: Identifying Angles

State Standards	Objective
• Math.Content.5-8 Geometry	• Identify parts of angles. • Identify types of angles.

Vocabulary
acute angle, angle, arc, end point, degrees, exterior, full rotation angle, interior, obtuse angle, protractor, reflex angle, right angle, sides, straight angle, vertex

Overview
An **angle** is formed by two lines, segments, or rays that share a common end point. Angles have two characteristics. All angles have a vertex. The **endpoint** that is shared by two rays that meet to form an angle is called a **vertex**. All angles have two **sides** or arms made from two line segments, rays, or lines. The symbol used to represent an angle is ∠. A **protractor** is an instrument used to measure angles. Protractors measure angles in **degrees** (°). The inside of an angle is called the **interior**. The outside of an angle is called the **exterior**.

Parts of an Angle   Angles are often but not always marked using an **arc** or segment of a circle.

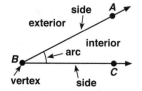

The correct way to name an angle is either to write *angle ABC*, ∠*ABC*, ∠*CBA*, or ∠*B*. The middle letter of the three is always the vertex.

Types of Angles

acute angle	right angle	obtuse angle
an angle with a measure greater than 0° and less than 90°	an angle that measures 90°	an angle with a measure greater than 90° but less than 180°
straight angle	**reflex angle**	**full rotation angle**
an angle that measures 180°	an angle that is greater than 180° but less than 360°	an angle whose measure is exactly 360°

Problems to Try

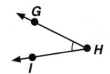

1. Name the angle.
2. Name the sides.
3. Name the vertex.
4. Name the type of angle.

Answer 1: ∠GHI, ∠IHG, ∠H
Answer 2: $\overrightarrow{GH}$ and $\overrightarrow{IH}$
Answer 3: Point *H*
Answer 4: acute angle

Real-World Connection
If you look around, you can see angles everywhere, from a slice of pizza to the edge of your desk.

Name: _____   Date: _____

Practice: Identifying Angles

Write *acute, right,* or *obtuse* to describe each angle.

1.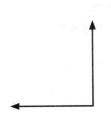

_____

2.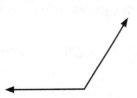

_____

3.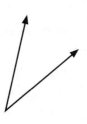

_____

Write *straight, reflex,* or *full rotation* to describe each angle.

4.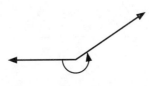

_____

5.

_____

6.

_____

Use the angle below to answer questions 7–10.   Use the figure below to answer questions 11–14.

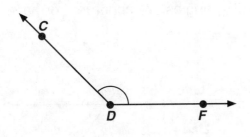

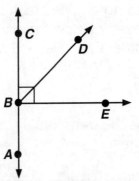

7. Name the vertex. _____

8. Name the angle. _____

9. Name the type of angle. _____

10. Name the sides. _____

11. Name an acute angle. _____

12. Name a right angle. _____

13. Name a straight angle. _____

14. Name an obtuse angle. _____

Lesson Introduction: The Transversal and Angles

State Standards	Objective
• Math.Content.5-8 Geometry	• Analyze relationship between transversal and angles.

Vocabulary
alternate exterior angles, alternate interior angles, angle, corresponding angles, congruent, transversal

Overview
An **angle** is formed by two lines, segments, or rays that share a common end point. The symbol for angle is ∠. When two parallel lines are crossed by a third line, special angle relationships exist.

1. The line that crosses the two parallel lines is known as the **transversal**. In the diagram to the right, lines x and y are parallel, and line t is the transversal. There are eight angles created and they are numbered 1 through 8.

2. **Alternate exterior angles** are the angles that lie on the outside of the parallel lines and on the opposite sides of the transversal. Alternate exterior angles are **congruent** or have the same measure. Example: ∠1 and ∠8

3. **Alternate interior angles** are the angles that lie on the inside of the parallel lines and on the opposite sides of the transversal. Alternate interior angles are congruent or have the same measure. Example: ∠3 and ∠6

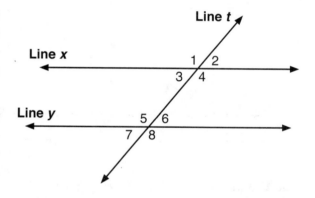

4. **Corresponding angles** are the angles that lie on the same side of the transversal and either both lie above or below the parallel lines. Corresponding angles are congruent or have the same measure. Example: ∠2 and ∠6.

Problems to Try

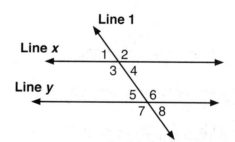

1. Which line is the transversal?
   Answer: Line 1

2. Name the corresponding angles.
   Answer: ∠1 and ∠5, ∠2 and ∠6, ∠3 and ∠7, or ∠4 and ∠8

Real-World Connection
The lines painted on the pavement in a parking lot are an example of parallel lines cut by a transversal.

Name: _____   Date: _____

Practice: The Transversal and Angles

Use the figure below to answer the questions.

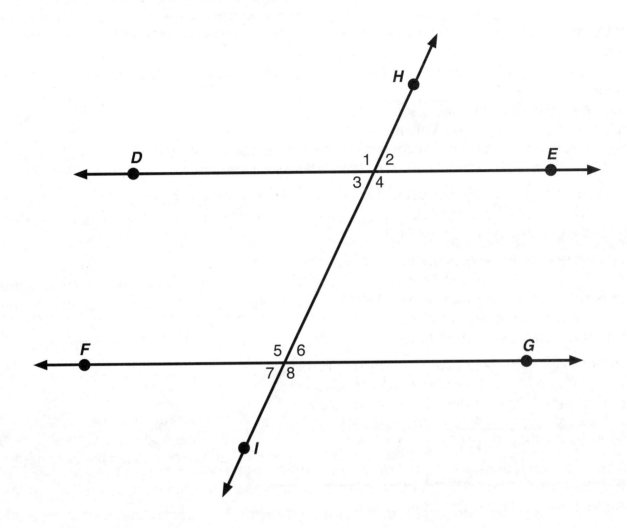

1. Name the transversal line. _____

2. List all interior angles. _____

3. List all exterior angles. _____

4. List all alternate exterior angles. _____

5. List all alternate interior angles. _____

6. List all corresponding angles. _____

Lesson Introduction: Measuring Angles

State Standards	Objective
• Math.Content.5-8 Geometry	• Use a protractor to measure angles.

Vocabulary
angle, degree, end point, measure, protractor, vertex

Overview
An **angle** is formed by two lines, segments, or rays that share a common **end point** or vertex. A **protractor** is an instrument used to measure angles. Protractors measure angles in **degrees** (°). One degree is written as 1°. Protractors are marked in degrees with one scale that is read clockwise and another scale that is read counterclockwise.

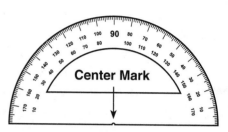

Measuring Angles With a Protractor

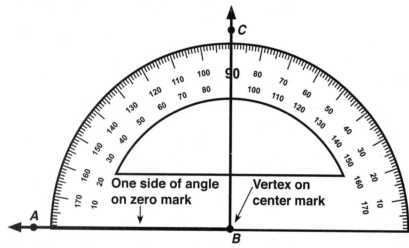

One side of angle on zero mark

Vertex on center mark

The center mark of the protractor is placed on the vertex of the angle. The endpoint that is shared by two rays that meet to form an angle is called a **vertex**.

To measure an angle, the base of the protractor is placed evenly on the line segment. One side of the angle must touch the zero mark.

The number of degrees in an angle is called its **measure** (m). To represent the measure of ∠ABC, we write m∠ABC = 90°.

Problems to Try

Find the measure in degrees of each angle.

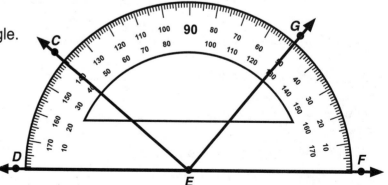

1. m∠DEC = _____ **Answer:** 40°

2. m∠DEG = _____ **Answer:** 130°

3. m∠GEF = _____ **Answer:** 50°

Real-World Connection
An air traffic controller uses geometry to determine the angles involved in a plane's flight path.

Name: _____   Date: _____

Practice: Measuring Angles

Use the protractor below to find the measure in degrees of each angle for questions 1 through 10.

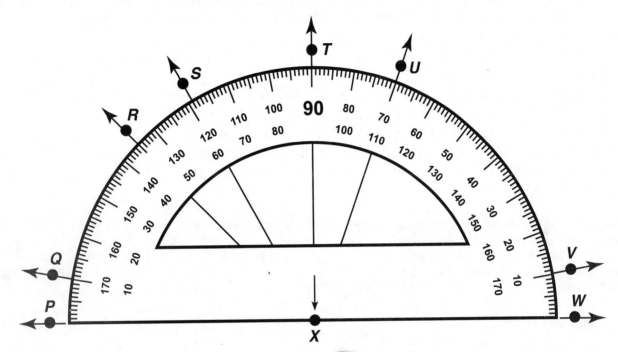

1. m∠PXQ = _____   2. m∠PXT = _____

3. m∠VXW = _____   4. m∠UXP = _____

5. m∠SXP = _____   6. m∠RXP = _____

7. m∠RXS = _____   8. m∠TXU = _____

9. m∠RXQ = _____   10. m∠WXQ = _____

Use a protractor to measure the angles.

11. _____   12. _____   13. _____

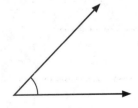
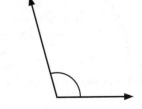
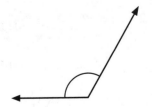

Lesson Introduction: More About Angles

State Standards	Objective
• Math.Content.5-8 Geometry	• Analyze characteristics and properties of angles.

Vocabulary

adjacent angles, exterior of an angle, interior of an angle, complementary angles, supplementary angles, vertical angle

Overview

The symbol for angle is ∠.

Terms	
Adjacent Angles *two angles that share a common vertex and a common side but do not have interior points that are the same; angle PQR and angle RQS are adjacent angles* 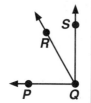	**Complementary Angles** *two angles whose measures total 90°; angles ABC and CBD are complementary* 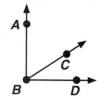
Exterior of an Angle 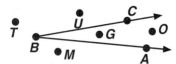 *the exterior is the set of points outside the angle; points T,U, and M are in the exterior of angle ABC*	**Supplementary Angles**  *two angles whose measures total 180°; angles JHK and JHI are supplementary*
Interior of an Angle 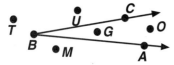 *the interior is the set of points inside the angle; points G and O are in the interior of angle ABC*	**Vertical Angle**  *an angle formed when two lines or line segments intersect; opposite vertical angles are congruent or equal; angles AOD and COB are vertical angles. Angles AOC and DOB are also vertical angles.*

Problems to Try

1. What is the missing angle measure for the supplementary angle? **Answer:** 45°

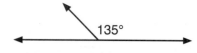

2. List all vertical angles.
   Answer: ∠1 and ∠3
   ∠2 and ∠4

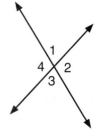

Real-World Connection

Every time you print the letter "X" you are forming vertical angles.

Name: _____   Date: _____

Practice: More About Angles

1. Write the name of the adjacent angles.

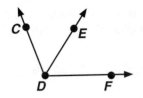

_____

2. Name the interior and exterior points in the angle.

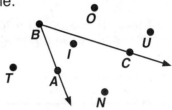

Interior Points _____

Exterior Points _____

Use the figure below to answer questions 3 through 9.

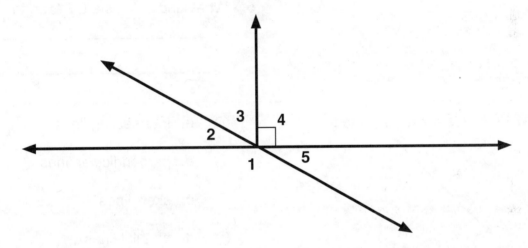

3. Name the supplementary angles. _____

4. Name the complementary angles. _____

5. Name the opposite vertical angles. _____

6. What is the measure of angle 4? _____

7. If angle 2 = 25°, what is the measure of angles 5, 3, and 1? _____

_____

8. If angle 3 = 60°, what is the measure of angles 2, 5, and 1? _____

_____

9. If angle 1 = 100°, what is the measure of angles 2, 5, and 3? _____

_____

Name: _____   Date: _____

Unit 1: Assessment

Fill in the bubble next to the correct answer for each multiple-choice question.

1. Lines *l* and *m* are parallel to one another and cut by transversal *t*. What is the value of *x*?

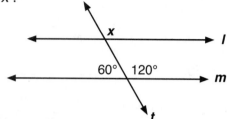

○ **a.** 60°

○ **b.** 40°

○ **c.** 120°

○ **d.** 75°

2. What kind of lines are represented?

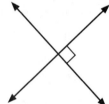

○ **a.** line rays

○ **b.** parallel lines

○ **c.** perpendicular lines

○ **d.** skew lines

3. Which angle equals 180°?

○ **a.** acute angle

○ **b.** right angle

○ **c.** straight angle

○ **d.** obtuse angle

4. What is the term for two angles whose measures total 90°?

○ **a.** supplementary angles

○ **b.** vertical angles

○ **c.** complementary angles

○ **d.** obtuse angles

5. What kind of lines are $\overleftrightarrow{PQ}$ and $\overleftrightarrow{RS}$?

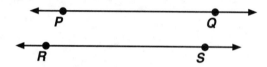

○ **a.** intersecting lines

○ **b.** perpendicular lines

○ **c.** skew lines

○ **d.** parallel lines

6. Which lines are skew?

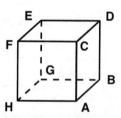

○ **a.** $\overleftrightarrow{EF}$ and $\overleftrightarrow{GH}$

○ **b.** $\overleftrightarrow{AB}$ and $\overleftrightarrow{CD}$

○ **c.** $\overleftrightarrow{ED}$ and $\overleftrightarrow{GH}$

○ **d.** $\overleftrightarrow{FC}$ and $\overleftrightarrow{HA}$

Name: _____   Date: _____

Unit 1: Assessment (cont.)

7. What type of angle is shown?

- ○ **a.** full rotation angle

- ○ **b.** acute angle

- ○ **c.** right angle

- ○ **d.** reflex angle

8. What kind of points are represented in the plane?

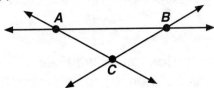

- ○ **a.** non-collinear points

- ○ **b.** coplanar points

- ○ **c.** collinear points

- ○ **d.** skew points

9. Which line is the transversal?

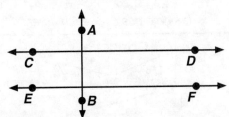

- ○ **a.** $\overleftrightarrow{EF}$

- ○ **b.** $\overleftrightarrow{CD}$

- ○ **c.** $\overleftrightarrow{AB}$

- ○ **d.** $\overleftrightarrow{DE}$

10. What is the measure of ∠JKL?

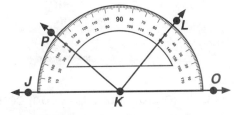

- ○ **a.** 50°

- ○ **b.** 130°

- ○ **c.** 40°

- ○ **d.** 140°

11. What is the missing angle measure?

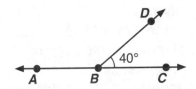

- ○ **a.** 120°

- ○ **b.** 140°

- ○ **c.** 110°

- ○ **d.** 80°

12. What kind of angle is represented?

- ○ **a.** right angle

- ○ **b.** acute angle

- ○ **c.** obtuse angle

- ○ **d.** straight angle

Lesson Introduction: Polygons

State Standards	Objective
• Math.Content.5-8 Geometry	• Identify properties of polygons. • Identify properties of simple and complex polygons.

Vocabulary

complex polygon, concave polygon, convex polygon, irregular polygon, polygon, regular polygon, sides, simple polygon, two-dimensional (2-D), vertex

Overview

A **plane** is an imaginary unlimited flat surface. It only has two dimensions, such as width and height, and no thickness. **Two-dimensional (2-D)** figures are called plane figures. A **polygon** is a two-dimensional (2-D),

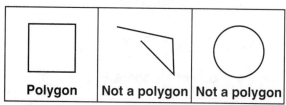

Polygon	Not a polygon	Not a polygon

closed figure that is formed by joining three or more line segments at their endpoints. Such shapes include squares, rectangles, triangles, and pentagons but not circles or any shape that includes a curve.

Parts of a Polygon

The **sides** are the straight line segments that make up the polygon. In **regular polygons**, all sides and angles are congruent. In **irregular polygons**, all sides and angles are not congruent.

The **vertex** (plural: vertices) is a corner of the polygon. In any polygon, the number of sides and vertices (end points) are always equal.

Each of the following is an example of a polygon:

Classifying Polygons

Simple	Regular	Complex
 *Sides do not cross over each other.*	 *All sides are congruent. All angles are congruent.*	 *Sides do cross over each other.*

Convex		Concave
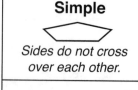 127° 67° 57° 111° *All vertices point outward. All interior angles are less than 180°.*		78° 48° 95° 214° 105° *One or more vertices point inward. One or more interior angles are greater than 180°.*

Problem to Try

Which figure is not a polygon?

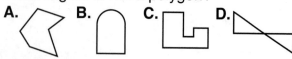
A.   B.   C.   D.

Answer: B

Real-World Connection

Artists such as painters and sculptors use the properties of shapes when creating artwork.

Name: _____   Date: _____

Practice: Polygons

Write *regular* or *irregular* for each polygon.

1.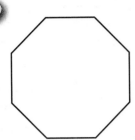

2.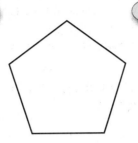

3.

4.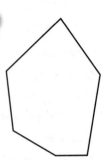

_____   _____   _____   _____

Write *simple* or *complex* for each polygon.

5.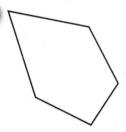

6.

7.

8.

_____   _____   _____   _____

Write *convex* or *concave* for each polygon.

9.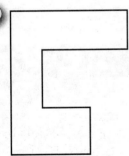

10.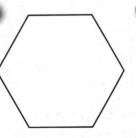

11.

12.

_____   _____   _____   _____

Lesson Introduction: Regular and Irregular Polygons

State Standards	Objective
• Math.Content.5-8 Geometry	• Identify regular polygons. • Identify irregular polygons.

Vocabulary

congruent, irregular polygon, polygon, regular polygon, two-dimensional (2-D)

Overview

A **two-dimensional (2-D)** shape has only two dimensions, such as width and height, and no thickness. A **polygon** is a two-dimensional, closed figure that is formed by joining three or more line segments at their endpoints. In some polygons, the lengths of the sides and/or sizes of the angles are congruent, or have the same measure.

Regular and Irregular Polygons

Regular Polygons: All sides are congruent, and all angles are congruent.			
Triangle: 3 sides	**Square:** 4 sides	**Pentagon:** 5 sides	**Hexagon:** 6 sides
Heptagon: 7 sides	**Octagon:** 8 sides	**Nonagon:** 9 sides	**Decagon:** 10 sides
Irregular Polygons: All sides are not congruent, and all angles are not congruent			
Quadrilateral	**Parallelogram**	**Trapezoid**	**Rectangle**

Problem to Try

Which figure is an example of an irregular polygon?

A.　　　　**B.**　　　　**Answer:** B

Real-World Connection

A stop sign is an example of a regular polygon.

Name: _____ Date: _____

Practice: Regular and Irregular Polygons

Write the name of each regular polygon.

1.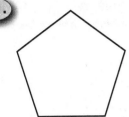

2.

3.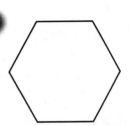

4.

_____   _____   _____   _____

Write the name of each irregular polygon.

5.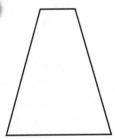

6.

7.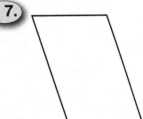

8.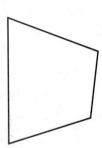

_____   _____   _____   _____

Write *regular* or *irregular* for each polygon.

9.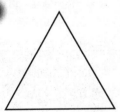

10.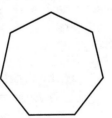

11.

12.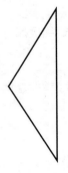

_____   _____   _____   _____

Lesson Introduction: Polygons Called Triangles

State Standards	Objective
• Math.Content.5-8 Geometry	• Identify triangles as polygons. • Identifying characteristics of triangles.

Vocabulary
congruent angles, congruent sides, interior angles, polygon, sides, triangle, vertices

Overview
A **polygon** is a two-dimensional, closed figure that is formed by joining three or more line segments called **sides** at their endpoints or **vertices**. **Triangles** are polygons that have three **interior angles** formed by three segments, or sides. In some, the length of the sides and/or size of the angles are the same measure. The symbol for angle is $\angle$.

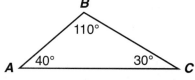

$\angle A + \angle B + \angle C = 180°$
The sum of the three interior angles of a triangle is always 180°.

Signs, Symbols, and Terms

Interior Angles	Points and Lines	Marking Angles
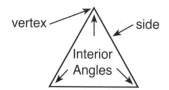	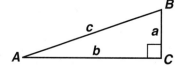	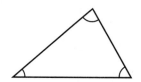
Angles are formed by joining three line segments called sides at their endpoints or vertices.	Points at the vertex are labeled with capital letters such as *A*, *B*, and *C*. Straight lines are often labeled with lower-case letters, such as *a*, *b*, and *c*.	Angles are commonly marked using an arc ($\frown$) or segment of a circle.
Marking Right Angles	**Congruent Angles**	**Congruent Sides**
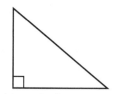	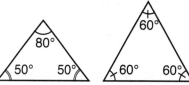	
A right angle (measures 90°) is marked with a square.	Congruent angles (same measure or angle size) are each marked with double arcs or tick marks (/).	Congruent sides (same length) are each marked with the same number of tick marks (/).

Problem to Try
Which of the following shows a triangle with three congruent sides?

A.　　　B.　　　C.　　　D.

Answer: D

Real-World Connection
A jeweler needs to know a lot about angles and geometry. There are specific geometric patterns that need to be followed when cutting diamonds into shapes.

Name: _____   Date: _____

Practice: Polygons Called Triangles

Write *side, vertex,* and *interior angles* to label 1 through 3 of the triangle.

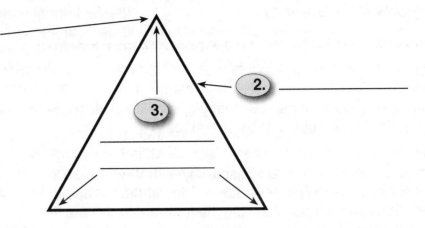

1. _____

2. _____

3.

_____

_____

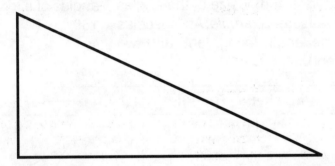

4. Mark the triangle to indicate a right angle.

5. What is the measure of a right angle? _____

6. What is the sum of the three interior angles of the triangle in #4? _____

7. What symbol is used to indicate a right angle? _____

8. What kind of letters are used to indicate points at the vertex? _____

9. Straight lines are often labeled with what kind of letters? _____

10. Double arcs or tick-marks are to indicate what kind of angles? _____

11. How are congruent sides marked? _____

12. What mark is commonly used to indicate angles? _____

13. What is the symbol for angle? _____

Lesson Introduction: Classifying Triangles

State Standards	Objective
• Math.Content.5-8 Geometry	• Identify triangles as polygons. • Classify triangles as right, acute, obtuse, scalene, isosceles, and equilateral.

Vocabulary

acute triangle, congruent, isosceles triangle, equilateral triangle, obtuse triangle, polygon, right triangle, scalene triangle, sides, triangle, vertices

Overview

A **polygon** is a two-dimensional, closed figure that is formed by joining three or more line segments called **sides** at their endpoints or **vertices**. **Triangles** are polygons that have three interior angles formed by three line segments, or sides.

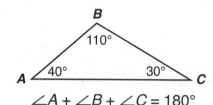

$\angle A + \angle B + \angle C = 180°$
The sum of the three interior angles of a triangle is always 180°.

Triangles are classified by the types of sides and angles they have. In some triangles, the length of the sides and/or size of the angles are **congruent**, or have the same measure. *Example:* An isosceles triangle has two sides with the same length (congruent) and two angles with the same size (congruent).

Classifying Triangles		
Right	**Acute**	**Obtuse**
one 90° angle *two acute angles* *(angles less than 90°)*	*all angles are less than 90°*	*one angle measures* *more than 90°*
Scalene	**Isosceles**	**Equilateral**
no congruent sides *no congruent angles*	*two sides congruent* *two angles congruent*	*all the sides congruent* *all the angles congruent*

Problem to Try

Which of the following shows a scalene triangle?

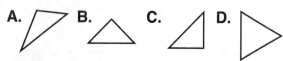

Answer: A

Real-World Connection

Architects use shapes and angles when drawing blue prints for residential, commercial, and public spaces.

Name: _____ Date: _____

Practice: Classifying Triangles

Write *right*, *obtuse*, or *acute* for each triangle.

 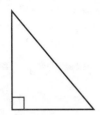   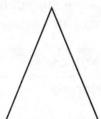 

_____ _____ _____ _____

Write *equilateral, isosceles,* or *scalene* for each triangle.

 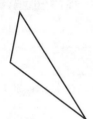      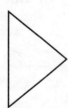 

_____ _____ _____ _____

9. Which of the following shows an equilateral triangle?

a. b. c. d.

10. Which of the following shows an isosceles triangle?

a. b. c. d.

Lesson Introduction: Find Unknown Interior Angle in Given Triangles

State Standards	Objective
• Math.Content.5-8 Geometry • Math.Content.5-8 Expressions and Equations	• Find the unknown interior angle in a given triangle.

Vocabulary

angle, congruent, equilateral triangle, interior angle, isosceles triangle, scalene triangle, triangle

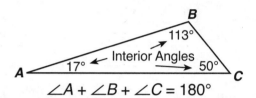

$$\angle A + \angle B + \angle C = 180°$$

Overview

Triangles are polygons. Every triangle contains three **interior angles**, angles inside the shape. Each angle is formed by two lines that share a common end point or **vertex**. The sum of the three angles is <u>always</u> 180°, no matter the size or shape of the triangle. The symbol for angles is ∠.

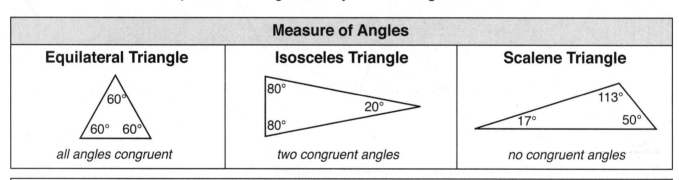

Measure of Angles		
Equilateral Triangle	**Isosceles Triangle**	**Scalene Triangle**
all angles congruent	*two congruent angles*	*no congruent angles*

Finding the Measure of a Missing Interior Angle

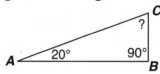

Step 1: Start with: $\angle A + \angle B + \angle C = 180°$
Step 2: Fill in measures you know. $20° + 90° + C = 180°$
Step 3: Rearrange and calculate. $C = 180° - 20° - 90°$
Step 4: Answer: $\angle C = 70°$

Problems to Try

1. What is the measure of missing angle *C*?
   Answer: $\angle C = 70°$

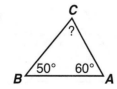

2. What is the measure of missing angle *A*?
   Answer: $\angle A = 55°$

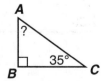

Real-World Connection

An artist creates a collage using lines, angles, and shapes.

Name: _____   Date: _____

Practice: Find Unknown Interior Angle in Given Triangles

Write the missing angle measure for each right triangle.

1.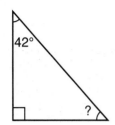

42°

?

2.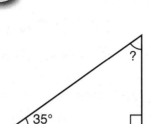

?

35°

3.

?

65°

4.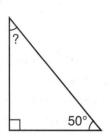

?

50°

_____   _____   _____   _____

Write the missing angle measure for each obtuse triangle.

5.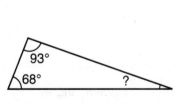

93°

68°

?

6.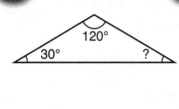

120°

30°   ?

7.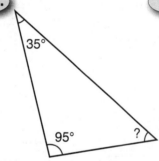

35°

95°   ?

8.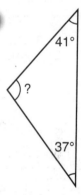

41°

?

37°

_____   _____   _____   _____

Write the missing angle measure for each acute triangle.

9.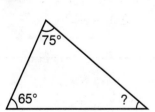

75°

65°   ?

10.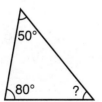

50°

80°   ?

11.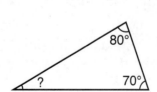

80°

?   70°

12.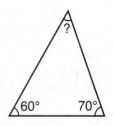

?

60°   70°

_____   _____   _____   _____

Lesson Introduction: Polygons Called Quadrilaterals

State Standards	Objective
• Math.Content.5-8 Geometry	• Identify quadrilaterals.

Vocabulary

congruent angles, congruent sides, interior angles, kite, parallelogram, polygon, quadrilateral, rectangle, rhombus, sides, square, trapezoid, vertices

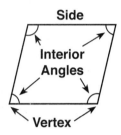

Overview

A **polygon** is a two-dimensional, closed figure. A **quadrilateral** is a polygon with four **sides** and four **vertices** or corners. The total of the **interior angles** (angles inside the shape) in any quadrilateral is always 360°. Some quadrilaterals have **congruent angles** (same angle measure) and **congruent sides** (have the same length).

Some quadrilaterals are also included in the definition of other types of figures. For example, a square, rhombus, and rectangle are also parallelograms. A square also fits the definition of a rectangle (all angles are 90°) and a rhombus (all sides are the same length).

Classifying Quadrilaterals		
Square	**Rectangle**	**Parallelogram**
4 sides equal length 4 interior right angles opposite sides are parallel	4 interior right angles opposite sides are parallel and congruent	opposite sides are parallel and congruent
Trapezoid	**Rhombus**	**Kite**
one pair of parallel sides	all sides have equal length opposite sides are parallel opposite angles are congruent	two pairs of adjacent sides that are congruent

Classifying Trapezoids

A quadrilateral with exactly one pair of parallel lines is a **trapezoid**. When the legs of the trapezoid are congruent (equal in length), it is an **isosceles trapezoid**.

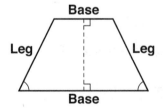

Problem to Try

Which of the following best describes the figure?

A. parallelogram   **B.** rhombus
C. square   **D.** trapezoid
Answer: D

Real-World Connection

A baseball diamond is a square 90 feet on each side with a 90° angle at each base pad.

Name: _____ Date: _____

Practice: Polygons Called Quadrilaterals

Write *kite, parallelogram, rectangle, rhombus, square,* or *trapezoid* to best describe each quadrilateral.

1.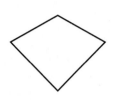

_____

2.

_____

3.

_____

4.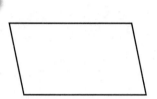

_____

5.

_____

6.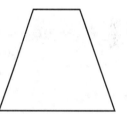

_____

For numbers 7 through 11, write all the letters from the figures that apply to each shape listed.

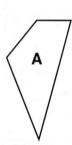

7. parallelogram _____

8. rectangle _____

9. rhombus _____

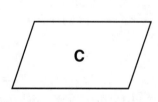

10. trapezoid _____

11. quadrilateral _____

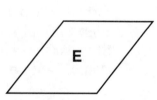

Lesson Introduction: Find Unknown Interior Angle in Given Quadrilaterals

State Standards	Objective
• Math.Content.5-8 Geometry • Math.Content.5-8 Expressions and Equations	• Find the fourth angle of a quadrilateral when the other three angles are known.

Vocabulary
angles, end point, parallelogram, polygon, quadrilateral, sides, vertices

Overview
A **polygon** is a two-dimensional (2-D), closed figure. A **quadrilateral** is a polygon with four **sides** and four **vertices** or corners. Each **angle** is formed by two lines that share a common **end point** or vertex.

Find Missing Measure of an Angle
The sum of the interior angles of a quadrilateral is equal to 360°.
$$\angle A + \angle B + \angle C + \angle D = 360°$$

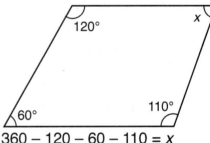

Simple Calculation
To find the fourth angle of a quadrilateral when the other three angles are known, subtract the number of degrees in the other three angles from 360°.

$$360 - 120 - 60 - 110 = x$$

Using an Equation
We can write an equation using the variable (x) and given measurements to figure out the measure of the unknown angle.

Step 1: Start with what you know.
Step 2: Fill in the known numbers
Step 3: Rearrange.
Step 4: Calculate.
Step 5: Answer

$$\angle A + \angle B + \angle C + \angle D = 360°$$
$$120 + 60 + 110 + x = 360$$
$$290 + x = 360$$
$$360 - 290 = x$$
$$70 = x$$

The unknown angle measure is 70°.

Problem to Try
What is the measure of the missing angle?

Answer: 125°

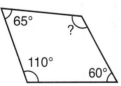

Real-World Connection
Designing cars involves knowing geometry. Engineers often use computers to help with the mathematical work for building prototype shapes and designs.

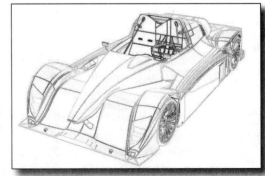

Name: _____   Date: _____

Practice: Find Unknown Interior Angle in Given Quadrilaterals

1. What is the sum of the angle measures of a quadrilateral? _____

Fill in the equations to find the missing angle measure (x) for each quadrilateral.

2.

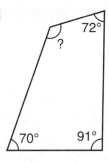

3.

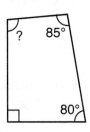

4.

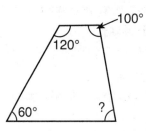

91 + _____ + 72 + x = 360	_____ + 80 + 90 + x = 360	120 + 100 + _____ + x = 360
_____ + x = 360	255 + x = 360	_____ + x = 360
360 − _____ = x	360 − _____ = x	360 − _____ = x
x = _____	x = _____	x = _____

Use the boxes below to write an equation using the variable (x) and given measurements to find the measure of the unknown angle.

5.

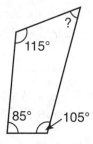

6.

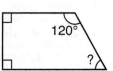

7.

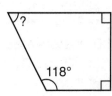

Lesson Introduction: Find Unknown Interior Angle in Given Parallelograms

State Standards	Objective
• Math.Content.5-8 Geometry • Math.Content.5-8 Expressions and Equations	• Find the unknown measures of parallelograms.

Vocabulary
angles, arc, congruent, parallelogram, sides, tick marks

Overview
A **parallelogram** is a quadrilateral where both pairs of opposite sides are parallel and are **congruent** (have the same measure), and opposite angles are congruent. A square and a rectangle are both parallelograms. In a parallelogram, the total of the interior angles is always 360°. The symbol for angle is ∠.

Finding Missing Length in a Parallelogram
Opposite sides are parallel and are congruent in length. The symbol ‖ means parallel. Sides *AD* are ‖ and sides *BC* are ‖. **Tick marks**, slashes (/) are used to identify sides with the same length. Angles are commonly marked using an arc (⌒) or segment of a circle.

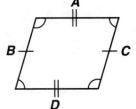

Find Missing Measure of an Angle

Square	Rectangle	Parallelogram

4 interior right angles 90° + 90° + 90° + 90° = 360°	4 interior right angles 90° + 90° + 90° + 90° = 360°	opposite angles are congruent ∠a = ∠d and ∠b = ∠c

Knowing the Measure of Only One Angle in a Parallelogram

The total of the interior angles is always 360°. ∠P + ∠Q + ∠R + ∠S = 360° 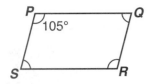	Start at any angle, and go around the parallelogram in either direction, each pair of angles you encounter are always supplementary—they add up to 180°. 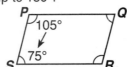	Opposite angles are congruent. ∠P = ∠R and ∠S = ∠Q 105 + 75 + 105 + 75 = 360° 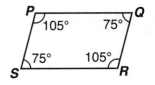

Problem to Try
What is the measure of the missing angle?

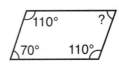

Answer: 70°

Real-World Connection
Geometry is important to a farmer planning how to divide his land for planting next year's crops.

Name: _____ Date: _____

Practice: Find Unknown Interior Angle in Given Parallelograms

Use tick marks (slashes) to indicate sides with the same length.

1.
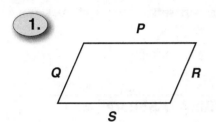

2.
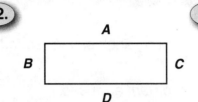

3.
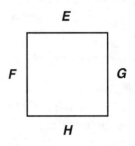

4. In a parallelogram, the total of the interior angles is always _____°.

Write the missing angle measure.

5.
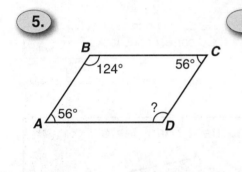

_____°

6.
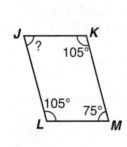

_____°

7.
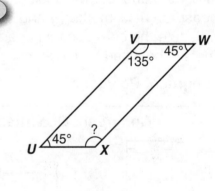

_____°

Write the measure of the missing angles.

8.
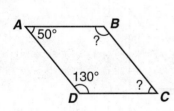

B = _____ C = _____

9.
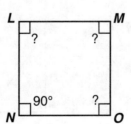

L = _____ M = _____

O = _____

10.
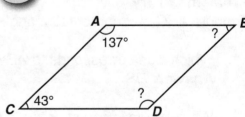

B = _____ D = _____

Lesson Introduction: Congruent or Similar?

State Standards	Objective
• Math.Content.5-8 Geometry	• Identify congruent figures. • Identify similar figures.

Vocabulary
congruent, congruent figures, corresponding angles, corresponding sides, similar

Overview
In geometry, the words *similar* and *congruent* are used to describe geometrical figures. **Similar** figures have the same shape, but can be different sizes. The **corresponding interior angles** are **congruent** (have the same measure) and the **corresponding sides** are proportional.

Congruent figures have the same size and the same shape. The corresponding sides have the same measure, and the corresponding angles have the same measure. Tick marks (/) and arcs (⌒) are often used to denote the corresponding parts of congruent figures. The symbol used to denote congruence is ≅.

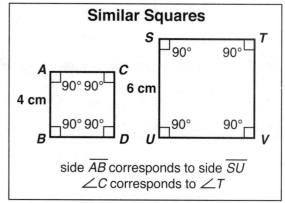

Similar Squares

side $\overline{AB}$ corresponds to side $\overline{SU}$
∠C corresponds to ∠T

Congruent Polygons

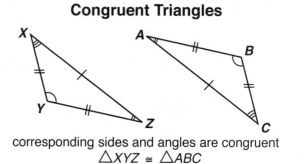

Congruent Quadrilaterals	Congruent Triangles
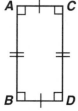 corresponding sides and angles are congruent rectangle *ABCD* ≅ rectangle *MNOP*	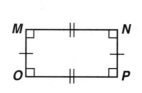 corresponding sides and angles are congruent △*XYZ* ≅ △*ABC*

Problems to Try
Triangle *ABC* is congruent to triangle *RST*.

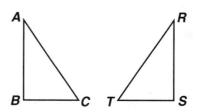

1. Which side corresponds to $\overline{AB}$?
   Answer: $\overline{RS}$

2. Which angle is congruent to ∠*BCA*?
   Answer: ∠*STR*

Real-World Connection
Congruent triangles are used in construction to reinforce structures.

Name: _____ Date: _____

Practice: Congruent or Similar?

Write *congruent* or *similar* for each set of figures.

1.

_____

2.

_____

3.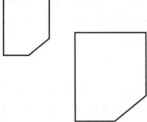

_____

4.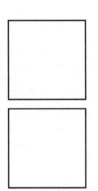

_____

5.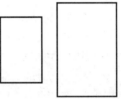

_____

6.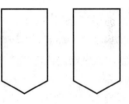

_____

Find the corresponding angles and sides for the two congruent triangles below.

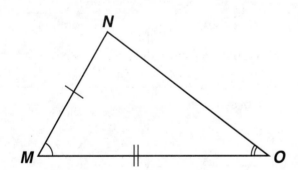 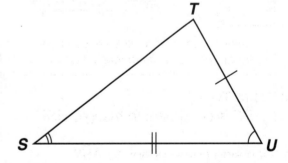

7. ∠M corresponds to ∠ _____

8. ∠N corresponds to ∠ _____

9. ∠O corresponds to ∠ _____

10. $\overline{MN}$ corresponds to _____

11. $\overline{NO}$ corresponds to _____

12. $\overline{OM}$ corresponds to _____

13. Which angle is congruent to ∠MON ? _____

Lesson Introduction: Lines of Symmetry

State Standards	Objective
• Math.Content.5-8 Geometry	• Identify lines of symmetry for figures.

Vocabulary
congruent parts, line of symmetry, symmetry

Overview
Symmetry occurs when two halves of a figure mirror each other across a line. The line that divides the figure into two mirror images is called the **line of symmetry**. The line of symmetry must separate the figure into two **congruent parts**, same size and shape. When the figure is folded over the line of symmetry, the two halves fit together. Some figures have more than one line of symmetry. The line of symmetry does not have to be vertical; it can go in any direction.

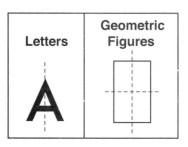

Letters	Geometric Figures

Lines of Symmetry in Polygons

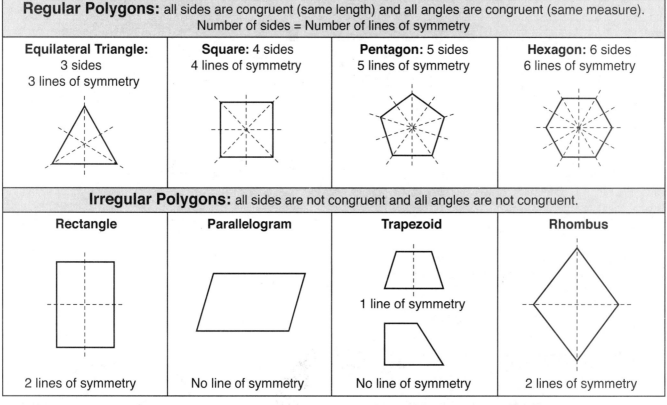

Regular Polygons: all sides are congruent (same length) and all angles are congruent (same measure).
Number of sides = Number of lines of symmetry

| **Equilateral Triangle:** 3 sides 3 lines of symmetry | **Square:** 4 sides 4 lines of symmetry | **Pentagon:** 5 sides 5 lines of symmetry | **Hexagon:** 6 sides 6 lines of symmetry |

Irregular Polygons: all sides are not congruent and all angles are not congruent.

| Rectangle | Parallelogram | Trapezoid | Rhombus |
| 2 lines of symmetry | No line of symmetry | 1 line of symmetry / No line of symmetry | 2 lines of symmetry |

Problem to Try
How many lines of symmetry does each figure have? **Answer:** A. 4, B. 1, C. 0

A.   B.   C.

Real-World Connection
Symmetric patterns occur in nature.

Name: _____   Date: _____

Practice: Lines of Symmetry

Write how many lines of symmetry there are in each of the regular polygons.

    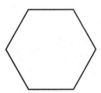

_____   _____   _____   _____   _____

Write how many lines of symmetry there are in each of the irregular polygons.

 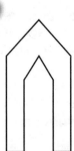  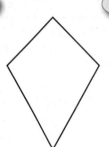 

_____   _____   _____   _____   _____

Draw the lines of symmetry for each figure.

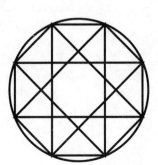  

Lesson Introduction: Transformations

State Standards	Objective
• Math.Content.5-8 Geometry	• Identify geometric transformations.

Vocabulary
rotation, reflection, transformation, translation

Overview
A **transformation** produces a copy, or image, of an original figure in a new position. There are three basic types of transformations: **translation** (slide), **reflection** (flip), and **rotation** (turn). After any of these transformations, the figure still has the same size, area, angles, and line lengths.

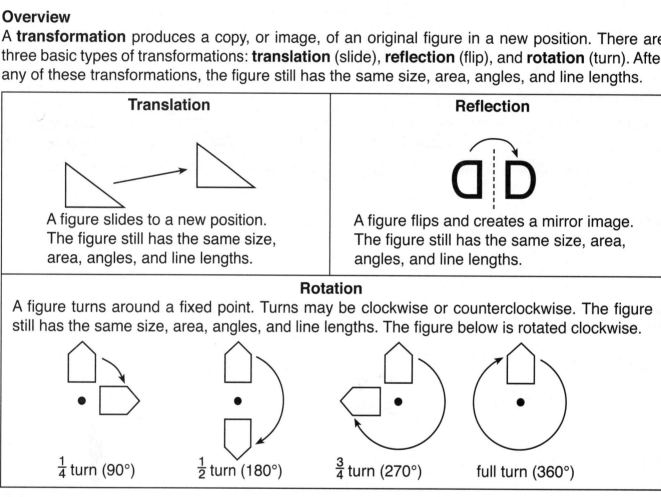

Translation

A figure slides to a new position. The figure still has the same size, area, angles, and line lengths.

Reflection

A figure flips and creates a mirror image. The figure still has the same size, area, angles, and line lengths.

Rotation

A figure turns around a fixed point. Turns may be clockwise or counterclockwise. The figure still has the same size, area, angles, and line lengths. The figure below is rotated clockwise.

$\frac{1}{4}$ turn (90°) $\frac{1}{2}$ turn (180°) $\frac{3}{4}$ turn (270°)   full turn (360°)

Problems to Try
Name each transformation.

1.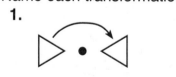

2.

3.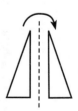

Answer: 1. rotation, 2. translation, 3. reflection

Real-World Connection
Geometry is used to create wallpaper designs. A design is translated or repeated many times in a specific direction.

Name: _____   Date: _____

Practice: Transformations

Write reflection, rotation, or translation for each transformation.

1.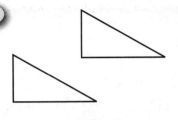

_____

2.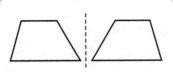

_____

3.

_____

Draw a translation of each figure.

4.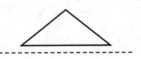

5.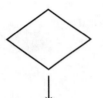

6.

Draw a reflection across the dashed line.

7.

8.

9.

Use the given degree to draw a clockwise rotation around the point for the following figures.

10. 90°

11. 180°

12. 270°

Name: _____   Date: _____

Unit 2: Assessment

Fill in the bubble next to the correct answer for each multiple-choice question.

1. Which figure is a polygon?

○ **a.**

○ **b.**

○ **c.**

○ **d.**

2. Which figure is an example of a regular polygon?

○ **a.**

○ **b.**

○ **c.**

○ **d.**

3. Which triangle shows a right angle?

○ **a.**

○ **b.**

○ **c.**

○ **d.**

4. Which of the triangles is an acute, equilateral?

○ **a.**

○ **b.**

○ **c.**

○ **d.**

5. What is the measure of the missing angle?

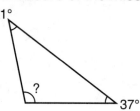

○ **a.** 95°

○ **b.** 112°

○ **c.** 102°

○ **d.** 98°

6. Which figure is a quadrilateral?

○ **a.**

○ **b.**

○ **c.**

○ **d.**

7. What is the measure of the missing angle?

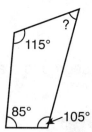

○ **a.** 60°

○ **b.** 55°

○ **c.** 85°

○ **d.** 105°

Name: _____   Date: _____

Unit 2: Assessment (cont.)

8. What is the measure of the missing angle?

○ **a.** 123°

○ **b.** 57°

○ **c.** 124°

○ **d.** 58°

9. What is the measure of the missing side?

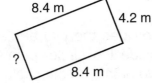

○ **a.** 42 m

○ **b.** 8.4 m

○ **c.** 4.2 cm

○ **d.** 4.2 m

10. Which pair shows two congruent figures?

○ **a.**

○ **b.**

○ **c.**

○ **d.**

11. Which pair shows two similar figures?

○ **a.**

○ **b.**

○ **c.**

○ **d.**

12. How many lines of symmetry are in the polygon?

○ **a.** 8

○ **b.** 5

○ **c.** 16

○ **d.** 4

13. What is the transformation?

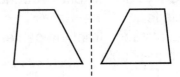

○ **a.** reflection

○ **b.** rotation

○ **c.** translation

○ **d.** 90° clockwise rotation

14. What is the transformation?

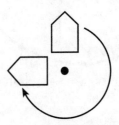

○ **a.** 90° clockwise rotation

○ **b.** 180° clockwise rotation

○ **c.** 270° clockwise rotation

○ **d.** 360° clockwise rotation

Lesson Introduction: Properties of Circles

State Standards	Objective
• Math.Content.5-8 Geometry	• Identify parts of a circle.

Vocabulary
arc, center point, central angle, chord, circle, circumference, diameter, plane, radius, sector

Overview
A **plane** is a flat surface that extends without end in all directions. A circle is the set of all points in a plane that are the same distance from its **center point**. A circle is named by its center. For example in the circle below, if point *B* is the center of the circle, then the name of the circle is circle *B*.

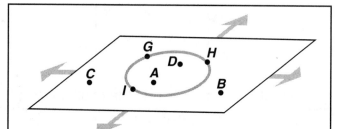

A circle divides the plane into three parts: points inside the circle, points outside the circle, and points on the circle.

Parts of a Circle

Circumference: the distance around the outer edge of a circle

Radius: the distance from the center of a circle to a point on the circle

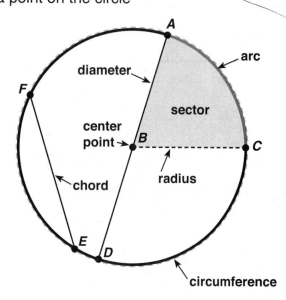

Diameter: the distance across a circle through its center point (The diameter is a chord that passes through the center point of a circle.); the diameter of a circle is twice as long as the radius

Chord: a line segment that connects one point on the edge of a circle with another point on the circle (Some chords pass through the center and some do not.)

Sector: a pie-shaped portion of the area of a circle

Arc: a line that links two points on a circle or curve

Central angle: an angle that has its vertex at the center of a circle; ∠*ABC* is a central angle of the circle shown at left; there are 360° in a circle

Real-World Connection
Pie charts use the parts of a circle to display information.

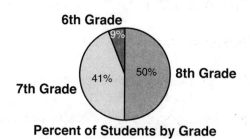

Percent of Students by Grade

Problems to Try
1. Name the center of the circle.
   Answer: Point *A*

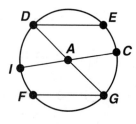

2. Name two chords on the circle that are not diameters.
   Answer: $\overline{DE}$ and $\overline{FG}$

Name: _____ Date: _____

Practice: Properties of Circles

Use the circle below to answer questions 1 through 4.

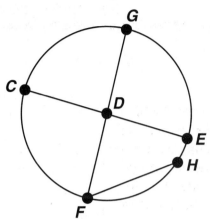

1. Name the center of the circle. _____

2. Name one chord. _____

3. Name two diameters. _____

4. Name four radii. _____

5. What is the total number of degrees for

the central angles shown? _____

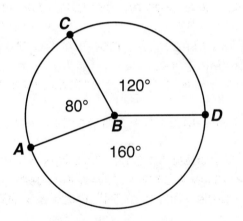

6. What is the measure of ∠SQT?

_____

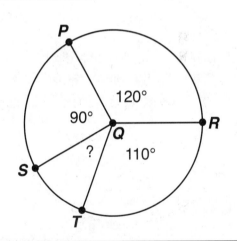

Write *circumference*, *diameter*, or *radius* to describe the items in 7 through 10.

7. The rim of a lens cap for a camera lens. _____

8. Spoke length of a bicycle wheel. _____

9. The distance around a tablecloth. _____

10. The distance across a circular plate. _____

Lesson Introduction: Find the Radius and Diameter of a Circle

State Standards	Objective
• Math.Content.5-8 Geometry • Math.Content.5-8 Expressions and Equations	• Identify the relationship between length of the radius and the diameter of a circle.

Vocabulary

center point, circle, diameter, plane, radius

Overview

A **plane** is a flat surface that extends without end in all directions. A **circle** is the set of all points in a plane that are the same distance from its **center point**. A circle is named by its center.

Radius	Diameter
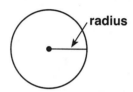	
Radius: a line segment with one endpoint at the center of the circle and the other endpoint on the circle; all radians of a circle are equal in length.	**Diameter:** the distance across a circle through its center point; the diameter of a circle is twice as long as the radius.

Finding Diameter

When given the radius of a circle, it is possible to calculate the diameter of that circle. The formula for finding the diameter of a circle is $d = 2 \cdot r$. The letter d represents diameter. The letter r represents radius. The symbol $\cdot$ means to multiply.

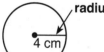

$$d = 2 \cdot r$$
$$d = 2 \cdot (4 \text{ cm})$$
$$d = 8 \text{ cm}$$

Problems to Try

1. Find the diameter of the circle.

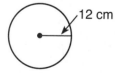

   Answer: $d = 24$ cm

2. Find the radius of the circle.

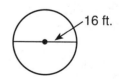

   Answer: $r = 8$ ft.

Real-World Connection

Gardeners often incorporate circles in their landscape designs.

Name: _____   Date: _____

Practice: Find the Radius and Diameter of a Circle

Find the diameter of each circle.

1.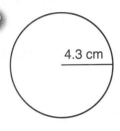
4.3 cm
_____

2.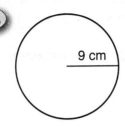
9 cm
_____

3.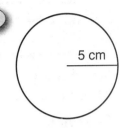
2.9 cm
_____

4.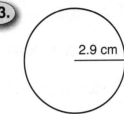
5 cm
_____

Find the radius of each circle.

5.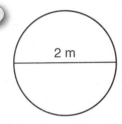
2 m
_____

6.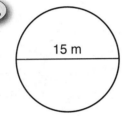
15 m
_____

7.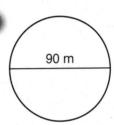
90 m
_____

8.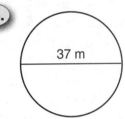
37 m
_____

9. Complete the table. Fill in the missing measures for radius and diameter.

Radius	4 cm	_____ cm	7 cm	8.5 cm	_____ cm	13.2 cm	_____ cm
Diameter	8 cm	11 cm	_____ cm	_____ cm	18 cm	_____ cm	28. 6 cm

10. Kimberly needs a jar lid. The diameter of the jar is 9 centimeters. Will a lid with a radius of 4 centimeters fit the jar? Explain your answer.

_____

_____

11. A circular pool has a radius of 13.5 feet. What is the diameter of the pool? _____

12. A bicycle wheel has a diameter of 22 inches. What is the radius? _____

Lesson Introduction: Circumference of a Circle

State Standards	Objective
• Math.Content.5-8 Geometry • Math.Content.5-8 Expressions and Equations	• Use formulas to solve problems involving circumference of a circle.

Vocabulary
circumference, diameter, pi, radius

Overview

$$\frac{C}{d} = \pi \approx 3.14$$

In the circle to the right, **C** stands for **circumference**, the distance around the circle; **r** represents **radius**, a line segment that joins the center of the circle with any point on its circumference; and **d** means **diameter**, a straight line passing through the center of a circle, ending at the circumference. For every circle, the ratio of circumference to diameter is the same. The ratio is approximately equal to 3.14 or $\frac{22}{7}$. This ratio is true for all circles. It is called **pi** and is represented by the Greek letter **π**.

Find Circumference

You can find the circumference if you know the diameter or radius of a circle. The formula is $C = \pi \cdot d$. The value used for pi is 3.14. Pi is a rounded number; therefore, answers will not be exact but approximate, or close. The symbol ≈ means the answer is approximate. The symbol • means to multiply.

Example: Diameter is 2 m

$C = \pi \cdot d$
$C \approx 3.14 \cdot (2 \text{ m})$
$C \approx 6.28 \text{ m}$

Example: Radius is 4 cm

Step #1: Find Diameter
$d = 2 \cdot r$
$d = 2 \cdot (4 \text{ cm})$
$d = 8 \text{ cm}$

Step #2: Find Circumference
$C = \pi \cdot d$
$C \approx 3.14 \cdot 8 \text{ cm}$
$C \approx 25.12 \text{ cm}$

Find Diameter and Radius

You can find the diameter and radius of a circle if you know the circumference.

Example: Circumference is 2,198 cm.

Step #1: Find diameter
$C = \pi \cdot d$
$2,198 \text{ cm} = 3.14 \cdot d$
$2,198 \text{ cm} \div 3.14 = d$
$d = 700 \text{ cm}$

Step #2: Find radius
$r = d \div 2$
$r = 700 \div 2$
$r = 350 \text{ cm}$

Problems to Try

1. Find the circumference.

7.6 cm

Answer: $C \approx 23.86$ cm

2. Find the circumference to the nearest tenth.

3.4 cm

Answer: $C \approx 21.4$ cm

3. Find the radius.

$C \approx 62.8$ m

Answer: $r = 10$ m

Real-World Connection

Mathematicians often use computers to make calculations. Using computers, they have calculated pi to over 1 trillion digits past the decimal point.

Name: _____   Date: _____

Practice: Circumference of a Circle

Find the circumference of each circle. Round answers to the nearest tenth.

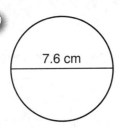

1.

7.6 cm

_____

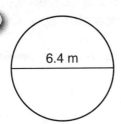

2.

6.4 m

_____

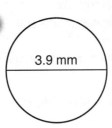

3.

3.9 mm

_____

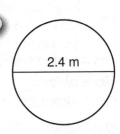

4.

2.4 m

_____

Find the circumference of each circle. Round answers to the nearest tenth.

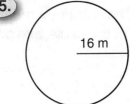

5.

16 m

_____

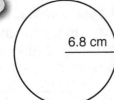

6.

6.8 cm

_____

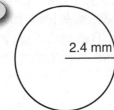

7.

2.4 mm

_____

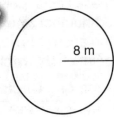

8.

8 m

_____

Solve the following word problems. Round answers to the nearest tenth.

9. The neighbor's above-ground circular swimming pool has a radius of 20 feet.

What is the circumference? _____

10. A circular tablecloth has a diameter of 8 feet. Joyce wants to sew lace around it to make it more decorative.

How many feet of lace will she need? _____

11. A medium pizza pan has a circumference of 120 cm. What is the pan's diameter?

_____

12. Jo's hula hoop has a circumference of 624 cm. What is the hoop's radius? _____

13. The track around the park is in the shape of a circle. The radius is 750 ft. Juan walked around the track once.

How far did he walk? _____

Lesson Introduction: Area of Circles

State Standards	Objective
• Math.Content.5-8 Geometry • Math.Content.5-8 Expressions and Equations	• Use formulas to solve problems involving area of circles.

Vocabulary
area, diameter, radius, pi, square units

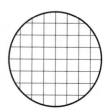

Overview
The **area** of a circle is the number of square units inside that circle. Area can be measured in **square units** (sq. units) such as square inches (in^2), square feet (ft^2), square centimeters (cm^2), or square meters (m^2). To find the area of a circle, multiply pi times the length of the radius squared. The formula for area is $A = \pi r^2$ or $A = \pi \cdot r \cdot r$. In the formula, **pi** is represented by the Greek letter π, and the value used for pi is 3.14. Pi is a rounded number; therefore, answers will not be exact but approximate, or close. The symbol $\approx$ means the answer is approximate. The **radius** is a line segment that joins the center of the circle with any point on the circle and is represented by the letter r. The symbol $\cdot$ means to multiply.

Area of a Circle

Example 1: Radius is 3 m	*Example 2:* Diameter is 8 m	*Example 3:* Area is 78.5 cm^2
		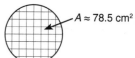
Formula: $A = \pi \cdot r^2$ $A = \pi \cdot r \cdot r$ $A \approx 3.14 \cdot (3\text{ m}) \cdot (3\text{ m})$ $A \approx 3.14 \cdot 9$ $A \approx 28.26\text{ m}^2$	Formulas: Step #1: Find Radius $d = 2 \cdot r$ $8\text{ m} = 2 \cdot r$ $8\text{ m} \div 2 = r$ $r = 4\text{ m}$ Step #2: Find Area $A = \pi \cdot r^2$ $A = \pi \cdot r \cdot r$ $A \approx 3.14 \cdot (4\text{ m}) \cdot (4\text{ m})$ $A \approx 3.14 \cdot 16$ $A \approx 50.24\text{ m}^2$	Formula: Find Radius $A = \pi \cdot r^2$ $A \approx 78.5\text{ cm}^2 = \pi \cdot r \cdot r$ $A \approx 78.5\text{ cm}^2 = 3.14 \cdot r \cdot r$ $A \approx 78.5\text{ cm}^2 \div 3.14 = r \cdot r$ $\sqrt{25}\text{ cm}^2 = \sqrt{r \cdot r}$ $r = 5\text{ cm}$

Remember: State your area answer with the correct units ($in.^2$, m^2, etc.).

Problems to Try

1. Find the area.

Answer: $A \approx 113.04\text{ m}^2$

2. Find the area.

Answer: $A \approx 78.5\text{ cm}^2$

3. Find the radius.

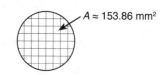

Answer: $r = 7\text{ mm}$

Real-World Connection
When you want to determine which pizza to order, it is helpful to know how to calculate the area of a circle to figure out which sizing option is the best value.

Name: _____   Date: _____

Practice: Area of Circles

Find the area of each circle. Round the answers to the nearest hundredth.

1. 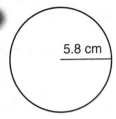 5.8 cm

_____

2. 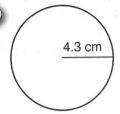 4.3 cm

_____

3. 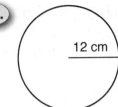 12 cm

_____

4. 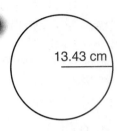 13.43 cm

_____

Find the area of each circle. Round the answers to the nearest hundredth.

5. 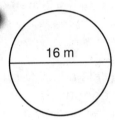 16 m

_____

6. 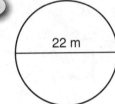 22 m

_____

7. 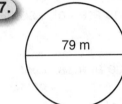 79 m

_____

8. 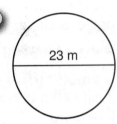 23 m

_____

Solve the following word problems. Round the answers to the nearest hundredth.

9. Tanya's circular flower bed has a diameter of 12 ft. What is the area of the flower bed?

_____

10. John's goat is tied to a post in the pasture. If the length of rope is 50 feet, what is the area of the pasture in which the goat can graze? _____

11. A local radio station broadcasts a signal over an area with a 65-mile radius. What is the area of the region that receives the radio signal? _____

12. An 18-inch pizza sells for $12.99. A 12-inch pizza sells for $6.99. Which size gives you more pizza for the money? Explain your answer. _____

_____

_____

Lesson Introduction: Area of Semicircles

State Standards	Objective
• Math.Content.5-8 Geometry • Math.Content.5-8 Expressions and Equations	• Use formulas to solve problems involving area of semicircles.

Vocabulary

area, semicircle, square units

Overview

The **area** of a circle is the number of **square units** inside that circle. The area can be measured in square units (sq. units) such as square inches (in²), square feet (ft²), square centimeters (cm²), or square meters (m²). To find the area of a circle, multiply pi (π) times the length of the radius (r) squared. The value used for pi is 3.14. Pi is a rounded number; therefore, answers will not be exact but approximate, or close. The symbol $\approx$ means the answer is approximate. A **semicircle** is half of a circle. Therefore the area of a semi-circle is $\frac{1}{2}\pi r^2$.

Parts of a Semicircle

Diameter (*d*) is the distance across a circle through its center point.
Remember: The diameter of a circle is twice as long as the radius.

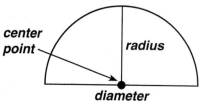

Radius (*r*) is a line segment with one endpoint at the center of the circle and the other endpoint on the circle.

Strategy for Finding Area of a Semicircle

Step #1: Find the radius of the semicircle.	**Step #2:** Find the area of the circle and divide by 2.
If you're only given the diameter (*d*) of the semicircle, you can divide it by two to get the radius (*r*). 14 cm $r = \dfrac{d}{2}$ $r = \dfrac{14}{2}$ $r = 7$ cm	Formula: $A = \frac{1}{2}\pi r^2$ $A \approx \frac{1}{2} \cdot 3.14 \cdot 7^2$ $A \approx 0.5 \cdot 3.14 \cdot 7 \cdot 7$ $A \approx 76.93$ cm² State your answer in square units.

Problem to Try

Find the area of the semicircle to the nearest tenth.

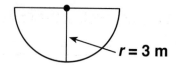

$r = 3$ m

Answer: $A \approx 14.1$ m²

Real-World Connection

A delicious example of a semicircle in real life is a hardshell taco.

Name: _____   Date: _____

Practice: Area of Semicircles

Find the area of each semicircle. Round the answers to the nearest hundredth.

1.
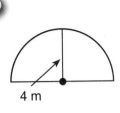
4 m

_____

2.
5.5 cm
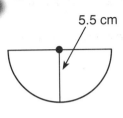

_____

3.
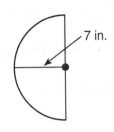
7 in.

_____

4.
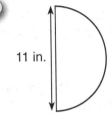
9 ft.

_____

5.
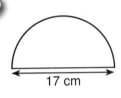
17 cm

_____

6.
26.4 m
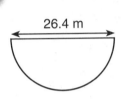

_____

7.
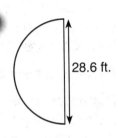
11 in.

_____

8.
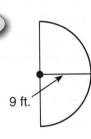
28.6 ft.

_____

Solve the following word problems. Round the answers to the nearest hundredth.

9. Joe has a pizza pie that has a diameter of 24 inches. If he cut it in half, what would be the area of half of his pizza pie? _____

10. Elsa makes and bakes large sugar cookies with a radius of 3 inches. She puts icing on half of each cookie. What is the area of the iced part of the cookie? _____

11. Connie's hot tub has a circular lid cover that hinges in the middle. The diameter of the lid cover is 2 meters. What is the area of half of the lid cover? _____

12. A circle drive is being paved. The drive area has a diameter of 45 meters. Half of the drive has been paved. What is the area of the paved part of the drive? _____

Name: _____   Date: _____

Unit 3: Assessment

Fill in the bubble next to the correct answer for each multiple-choice question.

1. What does $\overline{ST}$ represent?

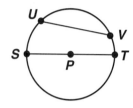

- ○ **a.** radius
- ○ **b.** center
- ○ **c.** diameter
- ○ **d.** arc

2. What is the measure of $\angle NMO$?

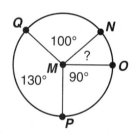

- ○ **a.** 30°
- ○ **b.** 40°
- ○ **c.** 80°
- ○ **d.** 20°

3. What is the diameter of a circle that has a radius of 6.5 cm?

- ○ **a.** 13 cm
- ○ **b.** 12.5 cm
- ○ **c.** 13 m
- ○ **d.** 6.5 cm

4. What is the radius of a circle that has a diameter of 90.6 m?

- ○ **a.** 40.3 m
- ○ **b.** 45.3 m
- ○ **c.** 45.6 m
- ○ **d.** 40.6 m

5. What is the circumference of the circle?

- ○ **a.** 94.2 ft.
- ○ **b.** 23.6 ft.
- ○ **c.** 32.7 ft.
- ○ **d.** 47.1 ft.

6. What is the circumference of the circle?

- ○ **a.** 47.1 m
- ○ **b.** 45.3 m
- ○ **c.** 94.2 m
- ○ **d.** 92.4 m

7. What is the circumference of a 12-inch diameter buttermilk pancake?

- ○ **a.** 37.7 inches
- ○ **b.** 36.7 inches
- ○ **c.** 18.8 inches
- ○ **d.** 17.8 inches

Name: _____   Date: _____

Unit 3: Assessment (cont.)

8. The distance around the merry-go-round is 62.8 ft. What is the radius?

○ **a.** 10 ft.

○ **b.** 8 ft.

○ **c.** 7 ft.

○ **d.** 6 ft.

9. What is the area of the circle?

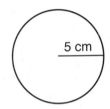

5 cm

○ **a.** 31.4 cm²

○ **b.** 78.5 cm²

○ **c.** 75.8 cm²

○ **d.** 34.1 cm²

10. What is the area of the semicircle?

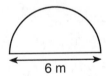

6 m

○ **a.** 18.84 m²

○ **b.** 56.52 m²

○ **c.** 14.1 m²

○ **d.** 28.2 m²

11. What is the radius of the circle?

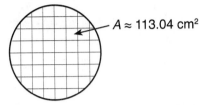

A ≈ 113.04 cm²

○ **a.** 12 cm

○ **b.** 8 cm

○ **c.** 6 cm

○ **d.** 3 cm

12. A lawn sprinkler sprays 4 yards in every direction as it rotates. What is the area of the sprinkled lawn?

○ **a.** 52.42 yds.²

○ **b.** 12.56 yds.²

○ **c.** 25.12 yds.²

○ **d.** 50.24 yds.²

13. A dinner plate has a radius of 8 centimeters. What is the area?

○ **a.** 50.24 cm²

○ **b.** 113.04 cm²

○ **c.** 200.96 cm²

○ **d.** 25.12 cm²

14. The diameter of a circular rug is 8 feet. What is the area?

○ **a.** 50.24 ft.²

○ **b.** 25.12 ft.²

○ **c.** 12.56 ft.²

○ **d.** 37.68 ft.²

Lesson Introduction: Three-Dimensional Figures

State Standards	Objective
• Math.Content.5-8 Geometry	• Identify properties of three-dimensional figures.

Vocabulary

area, edges, face, non-polyhedron, polyhedron, surface area, three-dimensional, vertex, vertices, volume

Overview

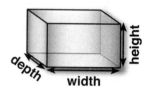

Solid geometry is the geometry of three-dimensional space. It is called **three-dimensional** (3-D) because there are three dimensions: width, depth, and height. Three-dimensional figures take up space or volume.

Examples of Three-Dimensional Figures

Properties of Three-Dimensional Figures

- **volume:** the measure of the amount of space inside of a solid figure
- **surface area:** the total surface area of all the faces and bases of a figure
- **vertices:** number of corner points

A **face** is the flat surface on a solid figure. Faces are in the form of plane shapes, such as triangles, rectangles, and squares.

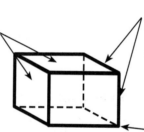

An **edge** joins one vertex with another. The dashed lines represent edges that are on the back side of the figure.

A **vertex** is a corner.

Types of Three-Dimensional Figures

There are two main types of solids: polyhedrons and non-polyhedrons.

Polyhedron (has all flat surfaces)	Non-Polyhedron (has surfaces that are not flat)

Problem to Try

Which is an example of a 3-D figure?

A.   B.   C.   D.

Answer: B

Real-World Connection

The ancient Egyptians built tombs in the shape of pyramids.

Name: _____   Date: _____

Practice: Three-Dimensional Figures

In order to describe 3-D figures, three special words are needed. Name the bolded part of each 3-D figure.

1.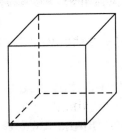

_____

2.

_____

3.

_____

Name the shape(s) of the faces in each figure.

4.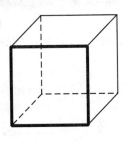

_____

5.

_____

6.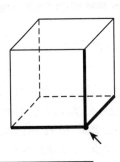

_____

7.

_____

Complete the table. Give the number of vertices, edges, and faces for each figure.

Figure	Number of Vertices	Number of Edges	Number of Faces
8.			
9.			
10.			

Lesson Introduction: Prisms

State Standards	Objective
• Math.Content.5-8 Geometry	• Classify prisms by their bases.

Vocabulary

base, edge, face, irregular prisms, lateral face, polyhedron, prism, regular prism, vertex

Overview

A **polyhedron** is a three-dimensional solid with flat sides or faces. The faces are all polygons.

A **prism** is a polyhedron with two parallel **bases** that are congruent polygons and faces that are parallelograms.

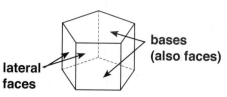

Faces, Edges, and Vertices

You can count the number of faces, edges, and vertices of a prism. A **face** is the flat surface on a solid figure. Faces are in the form of plane shapes, such as triangles, rectangles, and squares. **Lateral faces** are the flat surfaces that are not bases. An **edge** joins one vertex with another. A **vertex** is a corner. The dashed lines represent edges that are on the back side of the figure.

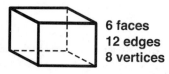

6 faces
12 edges
8 vertices

Types of Prisms

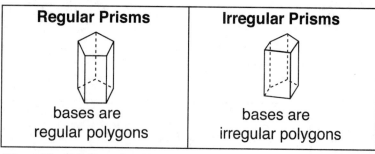

Regular Prisms	Irregular Prisms
bases are regular polygons	bases are irregular polygons

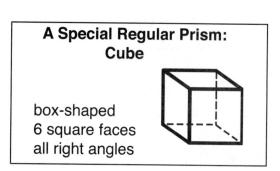

A Special Regular Prism: Cube

box-shaped
6 square faces
all right angles

Classify Prisms by Their Bases

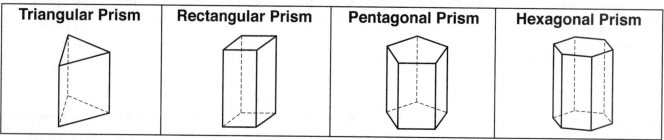

Triangular Prism	Rectangular Prism	Pentagonal Prism	Hexagonal Prism

Problem to Try

Identify the bases and lateral faces of the prism. Then name the figure.

Answer: Bases are pentagons.
Lateral faces are rectangles
The figure is a pentagonal prism.

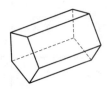

Real-World Connection

An ice cube is a small, three-dimensional piece of ice used to cool beverages. Ice "cubes" may be shaped like cubes, rectangular prisms, cylinders, and so on.

Name: _____   Date: _____

Practice: Prisms

The following table names and describes four kinds of prisms. Complete the table under number of vertices, edges, and faces. Name the shapes of the bases and lateral faces.

Kind of Prisms	Number of Vertices	Number of Edges	Number of Faces	Name of Bases	Name of Lateral Faces
1. Triangular Prism					
2. Rectangular Prism					
3. Pentagonal Prism					
4. Hexagonal Prism					

Lesson Introduction: Pyramids

State Standards	Objective
• Math.Content.5-8 Geometry	• Classify pyramids by their bases.

Vocabulary
base, edge, face, lateral face, polyhedron, pyramid, vertex

Overview
A **polyhedron** is a three-dimensional solid with flat sides or **faces**. The faces are all polygons. A **pyramid** is a polyhedron with triangles for **lateral faces** (faces that are not bases) and one **base**. The base can be any polygon. A pyramid is classified by the shape of the base.

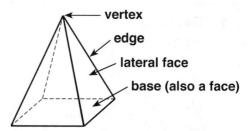

Faces, Edges, and Vertices
You can count the number of faces, edges, and vertices of a prism. A **face** is the flat surface on a solid figure. **Lateral faces** are the flat surfaces that are *not* bases. For a pyramid, the lateral faces are all triangles. An **edge** joins one vertex with another. A **vertex** is a corner. The dashed lines represent edges that are on the back side of the figure.

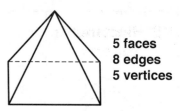

5 faces
8 edges
5 vertices

Classify Pyramids by their Bases

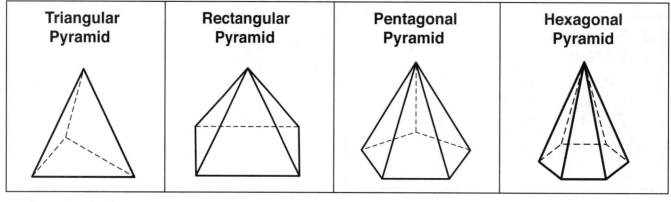

Triangular Pyramid	Rectangular Pyramid	Pentagonal Pyramid	Hexagonal Pyramid

Problem to Try
Identify the base and lateral faces of the pyramid. Then name the figure.

Answer: Base is a rectangle.
Lateral faces are triangles.
The figure is a rectangular pyramid.

Real-World Connection
Architects have designed pyramid-shaped buildings all around the world.

Name: _____   Date: _____

Practice: Pyramids

The following table names and describes four kinds of pyramids. Complete the table with the number of vertices, edges, and faces. Name the shapes of the bases and the lateral faces.

Kind of Pyramid	Number of Vertices	Number of Edges	Number of Faces	Name of Base	Name of Lateral Faces
1. Triangular Pyramid					
2. Rectangular Pyramid					
3. Pentagonal Pyramid					
4. Hexagonal Pyramid					

Lesson Introduction: Circular Objects

State Standards	Objective
• Math.Content.5-8 Geometry	• Identify properties of non-polyhedrons.

Vocabulary
base, cone, cylinders, edges, face, lateral face, non-polyhedron, polyhedron, right circular cylinder, sphere, three-dimensional, vertex

Overview
Solid geometry is the geometry of three-dimensional space. It is called **three-dimensional** (3-D) because there are three dimensions: width, depth, and height. Three-dimensional figures take up space or volume. There are two types of solid three-dimensional figures: polyhedrons and non-polyhedrons. A **polyhedron** is a three-dimensional solid with flat sides or faces. A **non-polyhedron** is a three-dimensional solid that has a curved surface (lateral face), not flat.

Faces, Edges, and Vertices
A **face** is the flat surface on a solid figure. **Lateral faces** are the flat surfaces that are not bases. A circular figure has one lateral face. The dashed lines represent edges that are on the back side of the figure.

Non-Polyhedrons

Right Circular Cylinder	Cone	Sphere
two opposite bases that are parallel and congruent, a curved surface (rectangle)	one circular base, a curved surface, a vertex that is opposite of the base	all its points are equal distance from the center point, a curved surface

Types of Cylinders
The most familiar type of **cylinder** is the **right circular cylinder** (above). It has a circular base. There are other kinds of cylinders. Cylinders can have bases other than circular shapes.

Examples of Other Cylinders	Examples of Other Cylinder Bases

Problem to Try
Give the number of bases, faces, edges, and vertices. Then name the figure.
Answer: 2 bases, 3 faces, 2 edges, 0 vertices; cylinder

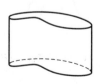

Real-World Connection
A soda can is a common everyday example of a non-polyhedron.

Name: _____   Date: _____

Practice: Circular Objects

The following table has examples of four non-polyhedrons. Complete the table with the number of vertices, edges, and faces.

Kind of Non-Polyhedrons	Number of Vertices	Number of Edges	Number of Bases	Number of Lateral Faces
1.				
2.				
3.				
4.				

5. Draw an example of a non-polyhedron that is not used in the table above.

6. Name two real-world examples of non-polyhedrons. _____

_____

Lesson Introduction: Platonic Solids

State Standard	Objective
• Math.Content.5-8 Geometry	• Identify properties of platonic solids.

Vocabulary
edge, face, platonic solids, three-dimensional, vertex

Overview
Solid geometry is the geometry of **three-dimensional** space. It is called three-dimensional (3-D) because there are three dimensions: width, depth, and height. Three-dimensional figures take up space or volume. There are two types of solid three-dimensional figures: polyhedrons and non-polyhedrons. **Platonic solids** are polyhedrons. Each **face** (flat surface) of a platonic solid is the same regular polygon. The same number of polygons meet at each **vertex** (corner). An **edge** joins one vertex with another. The dashed lines represent edges that are on the back side of the figure.

Classifying Platonic Solids

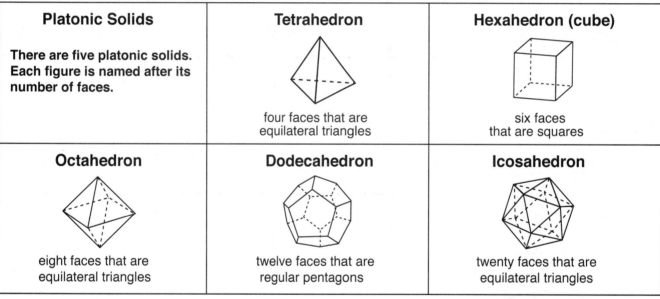

Platonic Solids	Tetrahedron	Hexahedron (cube)
There are five platonic solids. Each figure is named after its number of faces.	four faces that are equilateral triangles	six faces that are squares
Octahedron	Dodecahedron	Icosahedron
eight faces that are equilateral triangles	twelve faces that are regular pentagons	twenty faces that are equilateral triangles

Problem to Try
Which of the following is **NOT** a platonic solid?
- **A.** tetrahedron
- **B.** octahedron
- **C.** pentrahedron
- **D.** icosahedron

Answer: C

Real-World Connection
The tetrahedron, hexahedron (cube), and octahedron are found as crystals in nature.

Name: _____   Date: _____

Practice: Platonic Solids

The following table names and describes the five platonic solids. Complete the table with the number of vertices, edges, and faces. Name the shapes of the faces.

Platonic Solid	Number of Vertices	Number of Edges	Number of Faces	Name of Faces
1. Tetrahedron				
2. Hexahedron				
3. Octahedron				
4. Dodecahedron				
5. Icosahedron				

Lesson Introduction: Nets

State Standards	Objective
• Math.Content.5-8 Geometry	• Identify three-dimensional figures using nets.

Vocabulary
net, three-dimensional, two-dimensional

Overview
Shapes such as squares, circles, and triangles are **two-dimensional** figures. They only have two dimensions (such as width and height) and no thickness. They are also known as 2-D shapes. Solid shapes such as prisms and pyramids are **three-dimensional** (3-D) figures. They have three dimensions: width, depth, and height. A **net** is a two-dimensional pattern that can be folded to make a three-dimensional figure.

Nets
A net allows you to see all the surfaces of a three-dimensional shape at one time.

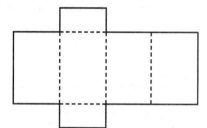 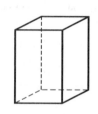

2 bases, rectangles
4 lateral faces, rectangles

A rectangular prism is formed by folding a net as shown.

Using Nets to Identify Figures
Step #1: Identify all the shapes that make up the net.
Step #2: Determine the number of bases and identify the shape of the bases.
Step #3: Identify the lateral faces (flat surfaces that are not bases).
Step #4: Visualize how the net is to be folded to form the solid.
Step #5: Name the shape.

Tips
Prisms are named by their bases. Pyramids are named by their bases. Cones have one circular base. Cylinders have two circular bases.

Problem to Try
Which is a net for a cone?

A.   B.   C.   D.

Answer: C

Real-World Connection
A soccer ball is made from a net. The pattern consists of 12 pentagons and 20 hexagons.

Name: _____ Date: _____

Practice: Nets

The following table depicts examples of nets. Complete the table with the number of bases and lateral faces. Name the shape of the bases and faces. Finally, identify what 3-D shape the net makes.

Net	Number of Bases	Number of Lateral Faces	What Shapes are the Bases?	What Shapes are the Lateral Faces?	What 3-D Object am I?
1. 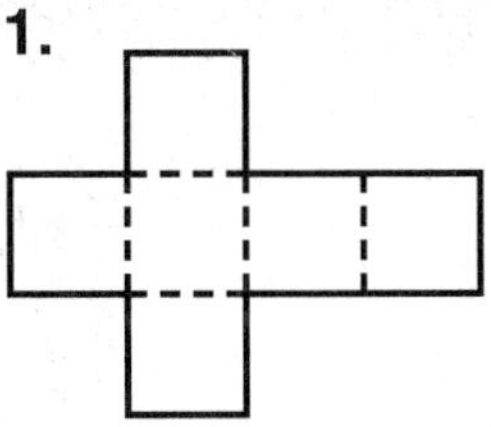					
2. 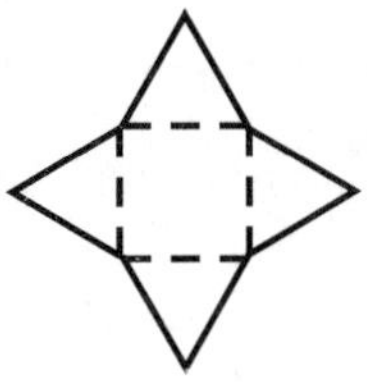					
3. 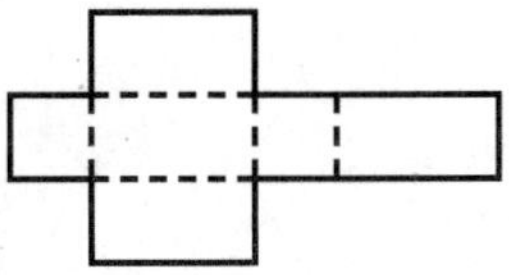					
4. 					
5. 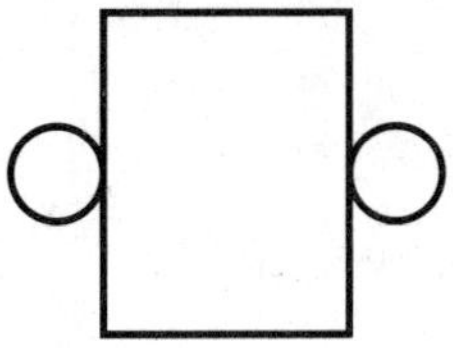					

Name: _____   Date: _____

Unit 4: Assessment

Fill in the bubble next to the correct answer for each multiple-choice question.

1. What is the name of the bolded part of the figure?

   ○ **a.** face

   ○ **b.** edge

   ○ **c.** vertex

   ○ **d.** side

2. What is the name of the lateral faces in the figure?

   ○ **a.** triangle

   ○ **b.** pyramid

   ○ **c.** rectangle

   ○ **d.** prism

3. How many vertices does the figure have?

   ○ **a.** 8

   ○ **b.** 5

   ○ **c.** 10

   ○ **d.** 6

4. What is the name of the bases in the figure?

   ○ **a.** pentagons

   ○ **b.** rectangles

   ○ **c.** octagons

   ○ **d.** hexagons

5. How many lateral faces does a rectangular pyramid have?

   ○ **a.** 4

   ○ **b.** 5

   ○ **c.** 6

   ○ **d.** 8

6. Which is an example of a non-polyhedron?

   ○ **a.**

   ○ **b.**

   ○ **c.**

   ○ **d.**

7. How many vertices does the figure have?

   ○ **a.** 2

   ○ **b.** 0

   ○ **c.** 1

   ○ **d.** 3

Name: _____   Date: _____

Unit 4: Assessment (cont.)

8. What is the name of the platonic solid?

    ○ **a.** tetrahedron

    ○ **b.** dodecahedron

    ○ **c.** octahedron

    ○ **d.** hexahedron

9. What is the name of the faces in the figure?

    ○ **a.** prisms

    ○ **b.** triangles

    ○ **c.** pyramids

    ○ **d.** rectangles

10. Which of the platonic solids has 8 vertices?

    ○ **a.**

    ○ **b.**

    ○ **c.**

    ○ **d.**

11. Which shows a net for a rectangular prism?

    ○ **a.**

    ○ **b.**

    ○ **c.**

    ○ **d.**

12. Which shows a net for a cylinder?

    ○ **a.**

    ○ **b.**

    ○ **c.**

    ○ **d.**

13. What solid figure could be made from the net?

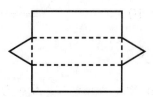

    ○ **a.** rectangular prism

    ○ **b.** triangular pyramid

    ○ **c.** square pyramid

    ○ **d.** triangular prism

Lesson Introduction: Perimeter of Polygons

State Standards	Objective
• Math.Content.5-8 Geometry • Math.Content.5-8 Measurement & Data	• Use formulas to solve problems involving perimeters of polygons.

Vocabulary
irregular polygon, perimeter, polygons, regular polygon

Overview
Perimeter (P) is the measure of the distance around an object. To find the perimeter, add the lengths of all sides. It can be measured in any standard distance measurement such as inches or centimeters. The answer is labeled with the measurement used in the problem.

In a **regular polygon**, where all the sides are congruent and all the interior angles are congruent, you can find the perimeter by multiplying the length of one side by the number of sides. In an **irregular polygon**, where all sides are not congruent and all angles are not congruent, add the lengths of all the sides to find the perimeter.

Finding Perimeter Using Formulas

Regular Polygons		
Equilateral Triangle	**Square**	**Regular Pentagon**
all sides are same length $P = a + a + a$ Or $P = 3a$	all sides are same length $P = a + a + a + a$ Or $P = 4a$	all sides are same length $P = a + a + a + a + a$ Or $P = 5a$

Irregular Polygons			
Triangle	**Rectangle**	**Trapezoid**	**Pentagon**
$P = a + b + c$	l = length, w = width $P = l + w + l + w$ Or $P = 2l + 2w$	$P = a + b + c + d$	$P = a + b + c + d + e$

Problem to Try
Find the perimeter of the figure.

Answer: $P = 12$ yd.

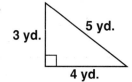

Real-World Connection
To build a fence around a yard, a property owner needs to find the perimeter of the yard to know how much fencing material to buy.

66

Name: _____   Date: _____

Practice: Perimeter of Polygons

Find the perimeter of each regular polygon.

1. 7 cm

_____

2. 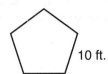 10 ft.

_____

3. 9 in.

_____

4. 6 in.

_____

Find the perimeter of each irregular polygon.

5.  10 cm   10 cm
8 cm

_____

6. 1 ft. 3 ft.

_____

7. 6 in. 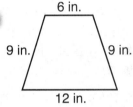 9 in.   9 in.   12 in.

_____

8. 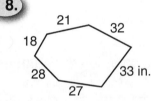 21   32   18   28   33 in.   27

_____

9. 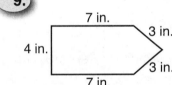 7 in.   3 in.   4 in.   3 in.   7 in.

_____

10. 13.62   13.95   15.75   14.78 in.   14.42

_____

Solve the following word problems.

11. Jillian is putting trim wire around her rectangular flower bed. The size of the flower bed is 4 ft. by 8 ft. How much trim wire does she need? _____

12. A square has sides that are 14.42 cm. What is the perimeter? _____

13. The perimeter of a rectangle is 32 yds. Its length is 6 yds. longer than its width. What is the length and width of the rectangle? Length = _____, Width = _____

14. A regular pentagon has 8 in. sides. A regular hexagon has 7 in. sides. Which regular polygon has the greatest perimeter? Explain your answer. _____

_____

_____

Lesson Introduction: Area of Irregular Regions

State Standards	Objective
• Math.Content.5-8 Geometry	• Estimate area of irregular figures.

Vocabulary
area, grid, square units

Overview
Area is the number of **square units** (units used to measure area) needed to cover the interior region of a plane, or flat, figure. Area can be measured in square units (sq. units) such as square inches (in.^{2}), square feet (ft.^{2}), square centimeters (cm^2), or square meters (m^2).

1 cm

1 cm

Each side of the square measures 1 centimeter. The area of the square is 1 square centimeter or 1 cm^2.

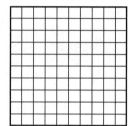

A **grid** is made up of squares. Each square measures 1 square unit.

Strategy for Estimating the Area of Irregular Regions

The area of a shape can be determined by placing that shape over a grid and counting the number of squares that the shape covers.

Step #1: Count full or almost full squares: 2
Step #2: Count squares that are almost half full: 8
Step #3: Do not count almost empty squares.
Step #4: Add the number of full squares plus the number of half-full squares
Step # 5: State your answer in square units. Use ≈ to indicate the answer is approximate.
  A ≈ 6 square units

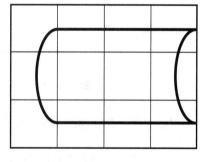

Problem to Try
Find the area of the irregular region.

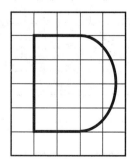

Answer:
$A ≈ 13$ square units

Real-World Connection
Conservation agents often have to find the area of lakes which cover irregular regions.

Name: _____   Date: _____

Practice: Area of Irregular Regions

Estimate the area of each irregular region in square units.

1.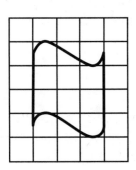

2.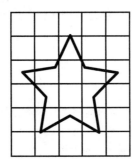

3.

$A \approx$ _____ square units $A \approx$ _____ square units $A \approx$ _____ square units

Draw an irregular shape on each grid. Estimate its area in square units.

4.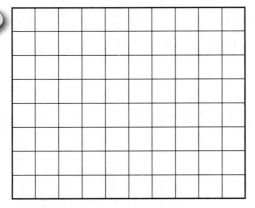

5.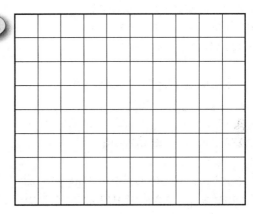

$A \approx$ _____ square units $A \approx$ _____ square units

Estimate the area of each figure, if each square unit is 1 sq. cm.

6.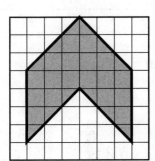

7.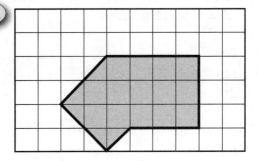

$A \approx$ _____ $A \approx$ _____

Lesson Introduction: Area of Triangles

State Standards	Objective
• Math.Content.5-8 Geometry • Math.Content.5-8 Expressions and Equations	• Use formulas to solve problems involving area of triangles.

Vocabulary
area, perpendicular, square units, triangle

Overview
The **area** of a polygon is the amount of surface the figure covers. The area can be measured in **square units** (sq. units) such as square inches (in.^{2}), square feet (ft.^{2}), square centimeters (cm^2), or square meters (m^2). A **triangle** is a three-sided polygon. To find the area of a triangle, multiply the base (*b*) by the height (*h*), and then divide by 2. The answer is stated in square units. The formula for the area of a triangle is:

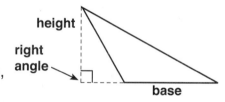

$$A = \tfrac{1}{2} \cdot b \cdot h \quad \text{or} \quad A = \frac{b \cdot h}{2}$$

In the formula for area, **b** is base and **h** is height. The symbol • means to multiply.

Finding Area Using a Formula

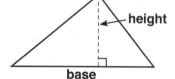

The base and height of a triangle must be perpendicular to each other and meet at 90 degrees to form a right angle. The base is a side of the triangle. However, depending on the triangle, the height may or may not be a side of the triangle.

Right Triangle	Acute Triangle	Obtuse Triangle
Solution:	Solution:	Solution:
$A = \tfrac{1}{2} \cdot b \cdot h$	$A = \tfrac{1}{2} \cdot b \cdot h$	$A = \tfrac{1}{2} \cdot b \cdot h$
$A = \tfrac{1}{2} \cdot (10 \text{ cm}) \cdot (10 \text{ cm})$	$A = \tfrac{1}{2} \cdot (8 \text{ yd.}) \cdot (7 \text{ yd.})$	$A = \tfrac{1}{2} \cdot (5 \text{ in.}) \cdot (12 \text{ in.})$
$A = \tfrac{1}{2} \cdot (100 \text{ cm}^2)$	$A = \tfrac{1}{2} \cdot (56 \text{ yd.}^2)$	$A = \tfrac{1}{2} \cdot (60 \text{ in.}^2)$
$A = 50 \text{ cm}^2$	$A = 28 \text{ yd.}^2$	$A = 30 \text{ in.}^2$

Problem to Try
Find the area of the triangle.
Answer: $A = 12 \text{ yd.}^2$

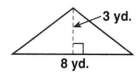

Real-World Connection
Professional painters may need to calculate the area of a triangle-shaped portion of a wall to determine how much paint they will need for a project.

Name: _____   Date: _____

Practice: Area of Triangles

Find the area of each triangle.

1.

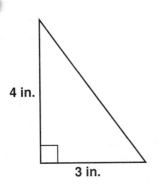

4 in.

3 in.

_____

2.

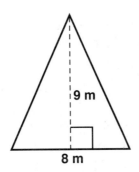

9 m

8 m

_____

3.

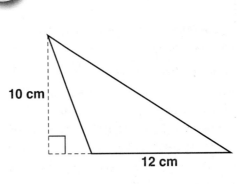

10 cm

12 cm

_____

4.

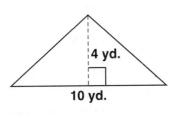

4 yd.

10 yd.

_____

5.

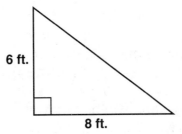

6 ft.

8 ft.

_____

6.

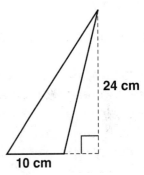

24 cm

10 cm

_____

7. The area of a triangle is 60 cm². If the height is 15 cm, what is the length of the base?

_____

8. The area of a triangle is 54 ft.². If the base is 9 ft., what is the height of the triangle?

_____

Lesson Introduction: Area of Quadrilaterals

State Standards	Objective
• Math.Content.5-8 Geometry • Math.Content.5-8 Measurement & Data	• Use formulas to solve problems involving area of quadrilaterals.

Vocabulary
area, base, perpendicular, polygon, quadrilateral, square units, vertices

Overview
A **quadrilateral** is a polygon with four sides and four **vertices** or corners. The **area** of a quadrilateral is the amount of surface the figure covers. The area can be measured in **square units** (sq. units) such as square inches (in.²), square feet (ft.²), square centimeters (cm²), or square meters (m²). When finding the area of quadrilaterals, the base and height must be **perpendicular** to each other, or meet at 90 degrees to form a right angle. The **base** is a side of the quadrilateral. However, depending on the quadrilateral, the height may or may not be a side.

Find Area Using a Formula
The area of a quadrilateral is stated in square units.

Quadrilateral	Formula
Rectangle	Area = $l \cdot w$ l = length, w = width The length and width are often referred to as "base" and "height," and sometimes the height is referred to as the "altitude."
Square	Area = $s \cdot s$ s = side The length and width are always the same number for a square; we usually call them "sides."
Parallelogram	Area = $b \cdot h$ b = base, h = height Sometimes the height is referred to as the "altitude."
Trapezoid	Area = $\frac{1}{2}(b_1 + b_2) \cdot h$ b_1 = base 1, b_2 = base 2, h = height Sometimes the height is referred to as the "altitude."

Problem to Try
Find the area of the square.

7 cm

Answer: $A = 49$ cm²

Real-World Connection
A painter calculates the area of a wall or ceiling to determine how much paint will be needed for a project.

Name: _____

Date: _____

Practice: Area of Quadrilaterals

Find the area of each quadrilateral.

1.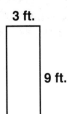
3 ft.
9 ft.

_____

2.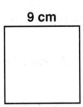
9 cm

_____

3.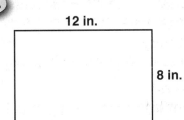
12 in.
8 in.

_____

4.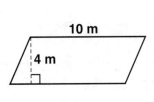
10 m
4 m

_____

5.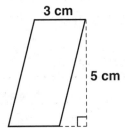
3 cm
5 cm

_____

6.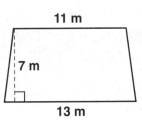
11 m
7 m
13 m

_____

7. Phillip is getting a new carpet for his room. The floor is 12 feet wide and 15 feet long. How many square feet of carpeting will he need? _____

8. The area of a rectangular rug is 760 square inches. The width of the rug is 20 inches. What is its length? _____

9. A parallelogram has a base that is 12 in. long and a height of 7 in. What is the area?

_____

10. A parallelogram has an area of 143 ft.². Its base is 11 ft. long. What is its height?

_____

Lesson Introduction: Area of Composite Figures

State Standards	Objective
• Math.Content.5-8 Geometry • Math.Content.5-8 Expressions and Equations	• Use knowledge of finding area of polygons to find the area of more complicated figures.

Vocabulary
area, composite figure, square units

Overview
A **composite figure** is made up of simple geometric shapes, such as semicircles, triangles, and rectangles. **Area** is the number of **square units** (units used to measure area) needed to cover the interior region of a figure. The area can be measured in square units (sq. units) such as square inches (in.^{2}), square feet (ft.^{2}), square centimeters (cm^2), or square meters (m^2).

Strategy for Finding Area of Composite Figures

Step #1: Divide the composite figure into two or more simple figures.	**Step #2:** Find the area of each simpler figure.

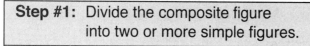

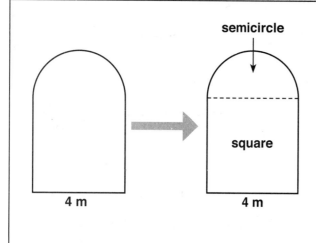

	Area of Semicircle **Area of Rectangle**
	Part A: Find Radius $A = b \cdot h$

Part A: Find Radius

$r = \dfrac{d}{2}$

$r = 4 \div 2$

$r = 2$

Part B: Find Area

$A = \pi \cdot r^2$

$A = \pi \cdot r \cdot r$

$A = 3.14 \cdot (2\ m) \cdot (2\ m)$

$A = 3.14 \cdot 4$

Divide by 2 for semicircle:

$A \approx 12.56\ m^2 \div 2$

$A \approx 6.28\ m^2$

Area of Rectangle

$A = b \cdot h$

$A = 4 \cdot 4$

$A = 16\ m^2$

Step #3: Add the areas of the simpler figures together. State your answer in square units.

$$A \approx 6.28 + 16$$
$$A \approx 22.28\ m^2$$

The value used for pi is 3.14. Pi is a rounded number; therefore, answers will not be exact but approximate, or close. The symbol ≈ means the answer is approximate.

Problem to Try
Find the area of the composite figure.
Answer: $A = 100$ ft.^{2}

8 ft.   12 ft.

10 ft.

Real-World Connection
Surveyors make precise measurements to determine property boundaries. When they are figuring out the area of a plot of land, they may divide it up into different shapes. Then they find the area of each individual shape and add up their answers to get the total area.

Name: _____   Date: _____

Practice: Area of Composite Figures

Find the area of each composite figure.

1.

3 cm

3 cm

2 cm

5 cm

_____

2.

10 m

6 m

15 m

_____

3.

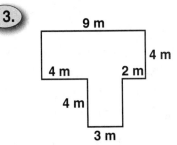

9 m

4 m

4 m

2 m

4 m

3 m

_____

4.

4 ft.

6 ft.

6 ft.

12 ft.

4 ft.

5 ft.

2 ft.

15 ft.

_____

5.

8 cm

10 cm

_____

6.

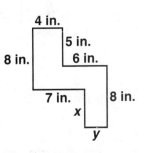

3 ft.

3 ft.

_____

List the measurements for each composite figure, including perimeter and area.

7. x = _____ yd.

y = _____ yd.

P = _____ yd.

A = _____ yd.^{2}

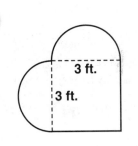

5 yd.

5 yd.

4 yd.

8 yd.

8 yd.

x

3 yd.

y

8. x = _____ in.

y = _____ in.

P = _____ in.

A = _____ in.^{2}

4 in.

5 in.

8 in.

6 in.

7 in.

8 in.

x

y

9. Loren is covering her patio with indoor/outdoor carpeting. Her patio is in the shape of a rectangle with a semicircle at both ends. The rectangle's dimensions are L = 12 ft. x W = 8 ft. How much carpeting will Loren need to complete the job?

_____

10. Karen is installing ceramic tile in her bathroom. Her bathroom is in the shape of a 5 ft. square connected to a 4 ft. x 5 ft. rectangle. How much ceramic tile will she need?

_____

Lesson Introduction: Surface Area of Prisms

State Standards	Objective
• Math.Content.5-8 Geometry • Math.Content.5-8 Expressions and Equations	• Use nets to solve problems involving surface area of prisms. • Use formulas to solve problems involving surface area of prisms.

Vocabulary
area, face, net, prism, square units, surface area, three-dimensional

Overview
A **three-dimensional** (3-D) figure has three dimensions: width, depth, and height. A **prism** is a three-dimensional figure with two parallel bases (faces) that are congruent polygons and faces (flat surfaces) that are parallelograms. The **surface area** (SA) of a prism is the total area of its faces. The area can be measured in **square units** (sq. units) such as square inches (in.^{2}), square feet (ft.^{2}), square centimeters (cm^2), or square meters (m^2). To see all the faces of a prism, use a net. A **net** is the pattern made when the surface of a three-dimensional figure is laid out flat, showing each face of the figure.

Strategy for Finding Surface Area of a Prism

Step #1: Draw a net of the shape if one is not provided in the problem.

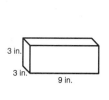

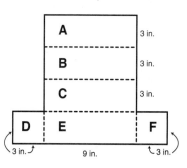

Label each face with a letter of the alphabet.

Step #2: Use a formula to calculate the area of each face. For a rectangular prism, use the formula $A = l \cdot w$.

A: $A = 9 \cdot 3 = 27$ B: $A = 9 \cdot 3 = 27$
C: $A = 9 \cdot 3 = 27$ D: $A = 3 \cdot 3 = 9$
E: $A = 9 \cdot 3 = 27$ F: $A = 3 \cdot 3 = 9$

Step #3: Add up the area of all the faces. State your answer in square units.

$$SA = 27 + 27 + 27 + 9 + 27 + 9$$

The surface area is 126 in.^{2}.

Problem to Try
Find the surface area of the triangular prism.

4 cm

5 cm   7 cm   8 cm

9 cm

Answer: $SA = 204$ cm^2

Real-World Connection
Box-manufacturing companies must calculate surface area to determine how much material they need for each box.

Name: _____   Date: _____

Practice: Surface Area of Prisms

Find the surface area of each prism.

1.

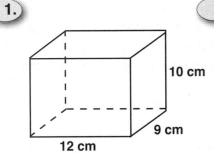

10 cm

9 cm

12 cm

_____

2.

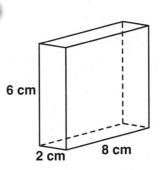

10 cm   14 cm

9 cm   20 cm

16 cm

_____

3.

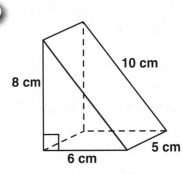

10 cm

8 cm

6 cm   5 cm

_____

4.

20 cm

4 cm

10 cm

_____

5.

6 cm

2 cm   8 cm

_____

6.

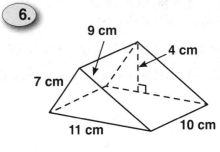

9 cm   4 cm

7 cm

11 cm   10 cm

_____

7. The aquarium in the classroom is in the shape of a rectangular prism. The base is 5 ft. by 2.5 ft. The height is 3 ft. How many square feet of glass was used to construct the aquarium?

_____

8. Tommy is painting the walls and ceiling of his new garage. It is 40 ft. long, 20 ft. wide, and 14 ft. high. What will be the area of the painted parts of his garage?

_____

Lesson Introduction: Surface Area of Pyramids

State Standards	Objective
• Math.Content.5-8 Geometry • Math.Content.5-8 Expressions and Equations	• Use nets to solve problems involving surface area of pyramids. • Use formulas to solve problems involving surface area of pyramids

Vocabulary

area, face, lateral faces, net, prism, square units, surface area, three-dimensional

Overview

A **three-dimensional** (3-D) figure has three dimensions: width, depth, and height. A **pyramid** is a three-dimensional figure with triangles for **lateral faces** (faces that are not bases) and one base. The **base** can be any polygon. The **surface area** (SA) of a pyramid is the total area of its faces. The area can be measured in **square units** (sq. units) such as square inches (in.²), square feet (ft.²), square centimeters (cm²), or square meters (m²). To see all the faces of a pyramid, use a net. A **net** is the pattern made when the surface of a three-dimensional figure is laid out flat, showing each face, including the base of the figure.

Strategy for Finding Surface Area of a Pyramids

Step #1: Draw a net of the shape if one is not provided in the problem.

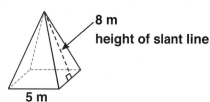

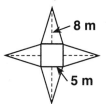

Step #2: Use a formula to calculate the surface area of each face. Start by finding the area of the base. In this problem, the base is a square. Next, find the total area of all the lateral faces.

Area of Base	Area of Triangle
$A = l \cdot w$	$A = \frac{1}{2} \cdot b \cdot h$ (slant line)
$A = 5 \cdot 5$	$A = \frac{1}{2} \cdot 5 \cdot 8$
$A = 25$ m²	$A = 20$ m²

Step #3: Find the total surface area by adding the area of the base and the total area of the lateral faces. State your answer in square units. (If it is a rectangular pyramid, each pair of sides will have a different area.)

$SA = 25 + 20 + 20 + 20 + 20$ or $SA = 25 + (4 \cdot 20)$ Surface area is 105 m²

Problem to Try

Find the surface area of the triangular pyramid.

Answer: $SA = 54$ m²

Real-World Connection

A large glass rectangular pyramid stands at the Louvre Art Museum in Paris, France.

Remember: The base is a triangle.

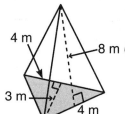

Name: _____   Date: _____

Practice: Surface Area of Pyramids

Find the surface area of each pyramid.

1.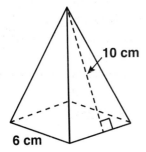
10 cm
6 cm

2.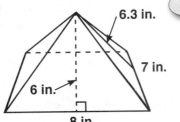
6.3 in.
7 in.
6 in.
8 in.

3.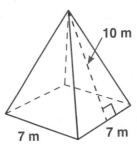
10 m
7 m   7 m

4.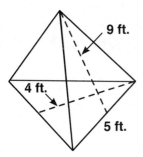
9 ft.
4 ft.
5 ft.

5.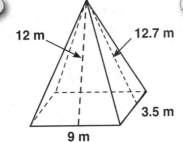
12 m   12.7 m
3.5 m
9 m

6.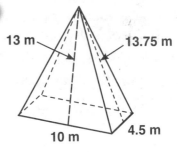
13 m   13.75 m
10 m   4.5 m

7. Dennis and Andy built a wooden pyramid with a square base of 25 feet and a slant height of 15 feet to use as a prop in the school play. Now they want to paint it. How much surface area do they need to cover? Assume they will paint the base of the pyramid.

_____

8. A large glass square pyramid is in the entranceway to the Louvre Art Museum in Paris, France. The base face has a side length of 35 meters. The pyramid's height is 21.6 meters. The slant line height of each triangular face is 28 meters. What is the total surface area of the pyramid? Include the area of the base.

_____

Lesson Introduction: Surface Area of Cones and Cylinders

State Standards	Objective
• Math.Content.5-8 Geometry • Math.Content.5-8 Expressions and Equations	• Use nets and formulas to solve problems involving surface area of cones and cylinders.

Vocabulary

base, cone, cylinder, face, lateral face, net, pi, radius, slant line, square units, surface area, three-dimensional

Overview

Cones and **cylinders** are **three-dimensional** (3-D) figures. They both have three dimensions: width, depth, and height. Both are three-dimensional solids with a curved surface (**lateral face**) that is not flat. The **surface area** (SA) of a cone or cylinder is the total area of the figure's faces. The area can be measured in **square units** (sq. units) such as square inches (in.^{2}), square feet (ft.^{2}), square centimeters (cm^2), or square meters (m^2). To see all the faces of a cone or cylinder, use a net. A **net** is the pattern made when the surface of a three-dimensional figure is laid out flat, showing each **face** of the figure.

Strategies for Finding Surface Area of a Cone and Cylinder

Step #1: Draw a net of the shape if one is not provided in the problem.

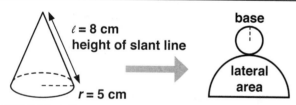

Step #2: Use a formula to calculate the total surface area of the figure.

The surface area (**SA**) of a cone is the area of the circular base (**B**) plus the lateral area (**L**). Use 3.14 for pi (π). The symbol (ℓ) stands for slant line height. The symbol ≈ means the answer is approximate, or close.

Formula:

$$SA = B + L$$
$$SA = \pi r^2 + \pi r \ell$$
$$SA \approx (3.14)(5^2) + (3.14)(5)(8)$$
$$SA \approx 78.5 + 125.6$$
$$SA \approx 204.1 \text{ cm}^2$$

State your answer in square units.

The surface area (**SA**) of a cylinder is two times the area of the circular base (**B**) plus the lateral area (**L**). Use 3.14 for pi (π). The symbol ≈ means the answer is approximate, or close.

Formula:

$$SA = 2B + L$$
$$SA = 2\pi r^2 + 2\pi r h$$
$$SA \approx 2(3.14)(2^2) + 2(3.14)(2)(5)$$
$$SA \approx 25.12 + 62.8$$
$$SA \approx 87.92 \text{ cm}^2$$

State your answer in square units.

Problem to Try

Find the surface area of the cylinder.

Answer: $SA \approx 43.96 \text{ m}^2$

Real-World Connection

Billions of food and beverage cans are manufactured every year. A cylinder shape takes less material to manufacture than cube-shaped containers.

Name: _____   Date: _____

Practice: Surface Area of Cones and Cylinders

Find the surface area of each cone. Round answers to the nearest hundredths.

1.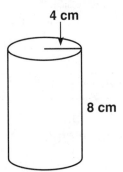
7 cm
$r = 6$ cm

_____

2.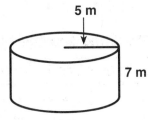
8.5 in.
$r = 3.5$ in.

_____

3.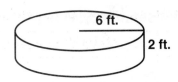
12 cm
$r = 9$ cm

_____

Find the surface area of each cylinder. Round answers to the nearest hundredths.

4.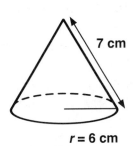
4 cm
8 cm

_____

5.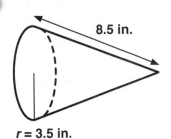
5 m
7 m

_____

6.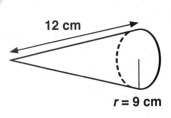
6 ft.
2 ft.

_____

7. Penny and Liam's grandfather told each of them to fetch him one of his canisters of oxygen. Penny's canister has a diameter of 7 inches and a height of 13 inches, Liam's has a diameter of 5 inches and a height of 20 inches. Whose canister has a larger surface area? Explain your answer.

_____

_____

8. Neal is making a cylindrical case to fit a bass drum with a height of 15 inches and a diameter of 24 inches. What is the surface area of the case?

_____

Lesson Introduction: Volume of Rectangular Prisms

State Standards	Objective
• Math.Content.5-8 Geometry • Math.Content.5-8 Expressions and Equations	• Find volume of a rectangular prism by counting cubic units. • Use a formula to solve problems involving volume of rectangular prisms.

Vocabulary

cubic unit, prism, rectangular prism, volume

Overview

The **volume** of a three-dimensional figure is the number of cubes it can hold. Each cube represents a unit of measure called a **cubic unit** (cu) such as cubic inches (in.^{3}), cubic centimeters (cm^3), or cubic meters (m^3). A **prism** is a three-dimensional figure with two identical ends and all flat sides. The prism is named after the shape of its base, so a prism with a rectangular base is called a **rectangular prism**.

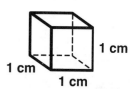

The cube measures 1 centimeter on each side. Its volume is 1 cubic centimeter (cm^3).

Find Volume of a Rectangular Prism

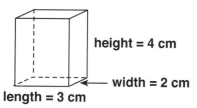

height = 4 cm

width = 2 cm

length = 3 cm

To find the volume of a rectangular prism, you can count cubes or calculate the area of the base and multiply it by the height. The formula is $V = Bh$ or $V = l \cdot w \cdot h$. The volume is 24 cm^3.

Strategy for Finding Volume of Rectangular Prisms

Step #1: Write down the formula for finding the volume of a rectangular prism.
Step #2: Find the area of the base and multiply it times the height.
Step #3: State your answer in cubic units.

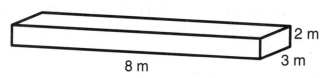

2 m

3 m

8 m

$V = Bh$
$V = B(\text{length of the base} \cdot \text{width of base}) \cdot h(\text{height of prism})$
$V = (3 \cdot 2) \cdot 8$
$V = 48 \text{ m}^3$

Problem to Try

Find the volume of the rectangular prism.

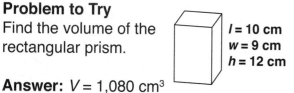

$l = 10$ cm
$w = 9$ cm
$h = 12$ cm

Answer: $V = 1,080$ cm^3

Real-World Connection

You might be amazed to know how much thought goes into designing the box for your favorite cereal. The manufacturer has carefully calculated how big a box needs to be to hold a certain amount of cereal.

Name: _____

Date: _____

Practice: Volume of Rectangular Prisms

Find the volume of each rectangular prism. Round answers to the nearest tenth.

1.

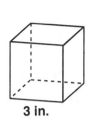

3 in.

2.

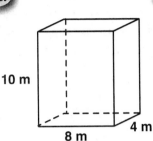

10 m

8 m   4 m

3.

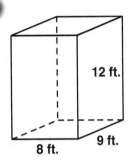

12 ft.

8 ft.   9 ft.

4.

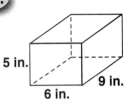

5 in.

6 in.   9 in.

_____   _____   _____   _____

5.

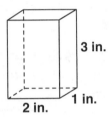

3 in.

2 in.   1 in.

6.

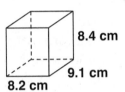

8.4 cm

8.2 cm   9.1 cm

7.

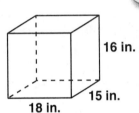

16 in.

18 in.   15 in.

8.

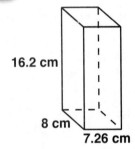

16.2 cm

8 cm

7.26 cm

_____   _____   _____   _____

9. Ben Green rented a building downtown for a new pet store business. Before he moves in, he must purchase an air-conditioning system to keep his pets cool. If the building is 32 ft. long, 30 ft. wide, and has a 10 ft. ceiling, what is the total volume of air he needs to cool?

_____

10. Jeremy drives a semi-truck that pulls a trailer. The trailer is a rectangular prism. The height of the inside of his trailer is 9 ft. The trailer is 8 ft. wide and 20 ft. long. What is the volume of his trailer?

_____

Lesson Introduction: Volume of Triangular Prisms

State Standards	Objective
• Math.Content.5-8 Geometry • Math.Content.5-8 Expressions and Equations	• Use a formula to solve problems involving volume of triangular prisms.

Vocabulary

bases, cubic unit, prism, triangular prism, volume

Overview

The **volume** of a three-dimensional figure is the number of cubes or partial cubes it can hold. Each cube represents a unit of measure called a **cubic unit** (cu) such as cubic inches (in.^{3}), cubic centimeters (cm^3), or cubic meters (m^3).

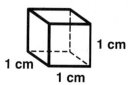

The cube measures 1 centimeter on each side. Its volume is 1 cubic centimeter (cm^3).

A **prism** is a three-dimensional figure with two identical ends (**bases**) and all flat sides. The prism is named after the shape of its base, so a prism with a triangular base is called a **triangular prism**.

Strategy for Finding Volume of a Triangular Prism

To find the volume of a triangular prism, calculate the area of one of the bases and multiply the answer by the height of the prism. The formula is Volume = Base • Height or $V = \frac{1}{2}$ length of one triangular base • height of one triangle base • height of one side of the prism.

Step #1:	Identify the length and height of one of the triangular bases. Identify the height (length of one side) of the prism. length of the base = 6 cm height of the base = 4 cm height of prism = 9 cm

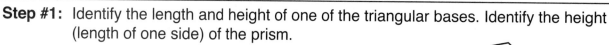

Step #2:	Write down the formula for finding the volume of a triangular prism. Find the area of the base. Then multiply the answer by the height of the prism. State your answer in cubic units. $V = Bh$ $V = B\,(\frac{1}{2} \cdot \text{length} \cdot \text{height of one triangle}) \cdot \text{height of prism}$ $V = (\frac{1}{2} \cdot 6 \cdot 4) \cdot 9$ $V = 12 \cdot 9$ $V = 108\ \text{cm}^3$

Problem to Try

Find the volume of the triangular prism.

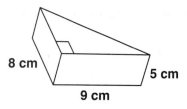

Answer: $V = 180\ \text{cm}^3$

Real-World Connection

Most products are shipped in boxes. The cost of a shipment can be affected by the amount of space that the box occupies. Cost is based on the volumetric (or dimensional) weight.

Name: _____   Date: _____

Practice: Volume of Triangular Prisms

Find the volume of each triangular prism.

1.

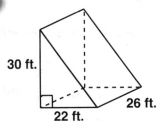

30 ft.

22 ft.

26 ft.

_____

2.

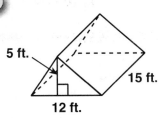

5 ft.

15 ft.

12 ft.

_____

3.

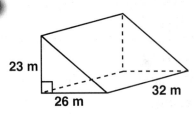

23 m

26 m

32 m

_____

4.

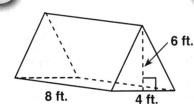

6 ft.

8 ft.

4 ft.

_____

5.

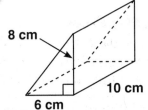

8 cm

10 cm

6 cm

_____

6.

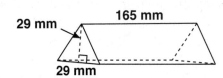

29 mm

165 mm

29 mm

_____

7. Hannah needs to mail a wall poster to her pen-pal in Spain. The poster is 22 inches long and has a rolled up diameter of 2 inches. She must select a box with the least volume to get the cheapest shipping rate. She has two choices: a rectangular prism with the dimensions: length = 23 in., width = 3 in., height = 3 in. or a box in the shape of a triangular prism with the dimensions: base length = 3 in., base height = 3.5 in., length of prism = 23 in. Which box should she choose to get the cheapest rate? Explain.

_____

_____

_____

Lesson Introduction: Volume of Cylinders

Standards State	Objective
• Math.Content.5-8 Geometry • Math.Content.5-8 Expressions and Equations	• Use a formula to solve problems involving volume of cylinders.

Vocabulary
cubic unit, cylinder, volume

Overview

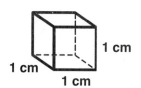

The **volume** of a three-dimensional figure is the number of cubes or partial cubes it can hold. Each cube represents a unit of measure called a **cubic unit** (cu) such as cubic inches (in.³), cubic centimeters (cm³), or cubic meters (m³). A **cylinder** is a three-dimensional figure with two parallel (usually circular) bases connected by a curved surface.

The cube measures 1 centimeter on each side. Its volume is 1 cubic centimeter (cm³).

To find the volume of a cylinder, multiply the area of the base by the height of the cylinder. The formula is: $V = Bh$ or $V = \pi r^2 h$.

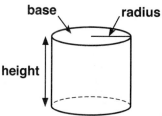

Strategy for Finding Volume of Cylinders

Step #1: Identify the radius and the height of the cylinder.	
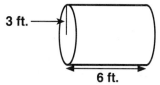	radius = 3 ft. height = 6 ft.
Step #2: Write the formula for volume of a cylinder. Use 3.14 for pi (π). Find the area of the base. Multiply the area of the base times the height. Round the answer to the nearest tenth. Use the symbol ≈ to show the measurement is approximate, or close. State your answer in cubic units.	$V = Bh$ or $V = (\pi r^2)h$ $V \approx (3.14 \cdot 3^2) \cdot 6$ $V \approx (3.14 \cdot 9) \cdot 6$ $V \approx 28.26 \cdot 6$ $V \approx 169.6$ ft.³

Problem to Try
Find the volume of the cylinder.
Answer: 141.3 m³

$r = 3$ m
$h = 5$ m

Real-World Connection
A cylinder is the most efficient use of material when manufacturing cans. They can hold the largest volume with the smallest surface area.

Name: _____   Date: _____

Practice: Volume of Cylinders

Find the volume of each cylinder.

1.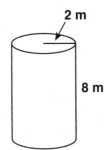

2 m

8 m

2.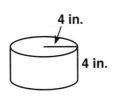

4 in.

4 in.

3.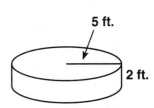

5 ft.

2 ft.

_____   _____   _____

4.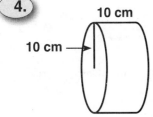

10 cm

10 cm

5.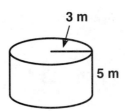

3 m

5 m

6.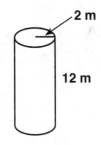

2 m

12 m

_____   _____   _____

Solve the following word problems. Round answers to the nearest hundredth, and use the approx-imate symbol ≈.

7. Noah's soda can is 5 inches tall and has a radius of 1.5 inches. What is the volume of soda in his can?

_____

8. James is filling a stock tank with water for his sheep. If the cylindrical tank has a diameter of 9 feet and a height of 3 feet, what is the volume of water the tank can hold?

_____

9. Megan has a cylindrical container that has a radius of 6 meters and a height of 2.1 meters. Sue's cylindrical container has a radius of 7 meters and a height of 0.7 meter. Whose container has the greater volume? Explain.

_____

_____

Name: _____   Date: _____

Unit 5: Assessment

Fill in the bubble next to the correct answer for each multiple-choice question.

1. What is the perimeter of a square with a length and width of 14.7 feet?

- ○ **a.** 58.8 feet

- ○ **b.** 216.09 feet

- ○ **c.** 29.4 feet

- ○ **d.** 56.9 feet

2. What is the perimeter of the figure?

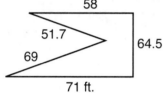

- ○ **a.** 312.4 feet

- ○ **b.** 245.2 feet

- ○ **c.** 314.2 feet

- ○ **d.** 262.5 feet

3. What is an area estimate of the figure?

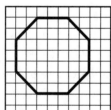

- ○ **a.** 31 square units

- ○ **b.** 51 square units

- ○ **c.** 33 square units

- ○ **d.** 41 square units

4. What is the area of the triangle?

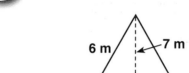

- ○ **a.** 36 m²

- ○ **b.** 21 m²

- ○ **c.** 43 m²

- ○ **d.** 29 m²

5. What is the area of the parallelogram?

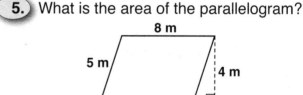

- ○ **a.** 40 m²

- ○ **b.** 20 m²

- ○ **c.** 32 m²

- ○ **d.** 17 m²

6. What is the area of the figure?

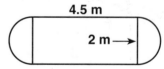

- ○ **a.** 56.52 m²

- ○ **b.** 24.28 m²

- ○ **c.** 12.14 m²

- ○ **d.** 31.8 m²

Name: _____   Date: _____

Unit 5: Assessment (cont.)

7. What is the surface area of the rectangular prism?

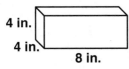

4 in.
4 in.
8 in.

- ○ **a.** 128 in.²
- ○ **b.** 160 in.²
- ○ **c.** 96 in.²
- ○ **d.** 144 in.²

8. What is the surface area of the pyramid?

7 m
6 m
6 m

- ○ **a.** 108 m²
- ○ **b.** 105 m²
- ○ **c.** 57 m²
- ○ **d.** 120 m²

9. What is the surface area of the figure?

2 m
1 m
11 m

- ○ **a.** 78.5 m³
- ○ **b.** 78.5 m²
- ○ **c.** 97.34 m³
- ○ **d.** 97.34 m²

10. What is the volume of the rectangular prism?

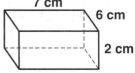

7 cm
6 cm
2 cm

- ○ **a.** 84 cm²
- ○ **b.** 84 cm³
- ○ **c.** 98 cm²
- ○ **d.** 98 cm³

11. Scott needs to know the volume of his house in order to purchase the right air-conditioning unit. What is the volume of his house?

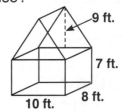

9 ft.
7 ft.
8 ft.
10 ft.

- ○ **a.** 920 ft.³
- ○ **b.** 920 ft.²
- ○ **c.** 1,280 ft.³
- ○ **d.** 1,280 ft.²

12. The farm supply store has a circular water tank that is 3 feet high and 8 feet across. What volume of water can it hold?

- ○ **a.** 150.7 ft.²
- ○ **b.** 602.9 ft.³
- ○ **c.** 150.7 ft.³
- ○ **d.** 602.9 ft.²

Glossary

acute angle: an angle with a measure greater than 0° and less than 90°

acute triangle: a triangle with all acute angles

adjacent angles: two angles that share a common vertex and a common side but do not have interior points that are the same

alternate exterior angles: the angles that lie on the outside of the parallel lines and on the opposite sides of the transversal

alternate interior angles: the angles that lie on the inside of the parallel lines and on the opposite sides of the transversal

angle: a corner formed by two lines, segments, or rays that share a common end point

approximate: not exact, but close; ≈ is the symbol for approximate

arc: a segment of a circle

area: the space occupied by a two-dimensional figure

base: the line or plane upon which a geometric figure is thought of as resting

center angle: an angle that has its vertex at the center of a circle

center point: a single point indicating the center of a circle

chord: a line segment whose endpoints are points on the circle

circle: a closed plane curve with each point in the curve at the same distance from a given interior point called the center

circumference: the distance around the outer edge of a circle

collinear points: points that lie on the same straight line

complex polygon: a two-dimensional figure with sides that do cross over each other

complementary angles: two angles whose measures total 90°

composite figure: a figure made up of simple geometric shapes, such as semicircles, triangles, and rectangles

concave polygon: a two-dimensional figure with one or more vertices that point inward; one or more interior angles is greater than 180°

cone: a three-dimensional figure with a circular base and the top meeting at a vertex; it resembles a funnel

congruent: the same shape and size

congruent parts: the parts of a figure that are the same size and shape

congruent segments: line segments that have the same lengths

convex polygon: a figure in which a line segment with endpoints in a simple closed figure contains no points in the exterior of the figure

coplanar lines: two lines in the same plane

corresponding angles: the angles that lie on the same side of the transversal and either both lie above or below the parallel lines

corresponding sides: sides with the same measure

cubic unit: a measure of volume; it is equal to the volume of a cube, which is one unit high, one unit wide, and one unit long

cylinder: a three-dimensional figure with two circular bases; it resembles a can

decagon: a ten-sided polygon

degree (°): the unit with which angles are measured

diameter: a chord (line segment) whose endpoints are collinear with the center of a circle; the center is between the endpoints of the diameter

dodecahedron: a polyhedron with twelve faces, which are regular pentagons

edge: the line segments that are the intersection of two faces of a space figure

endpoint: a single point indicating where a line segment or ray ends

equilateral triangle: a triangle with three congruent sides

exterior: the area outside of an angle

exterior angle: the angle between the side of a polygon and an extended adjacent side

face: a flat surface of a three-dimensional figure

full rotation angle: an angle whose measure is exactly 360°

geometry: a branch of math that focuses on the measurement and relationship of points, lines, angles, surfaces, and solids

heptagon: a seven-sided polygon

hexagon: a six-sided polygon

hexagonal prism: a prism with two hexagonal bases

hexagonal pyramid: a pyramid with a hexagonal base

hexahedron: a polyhedron with six faces that are squares; also called a cube

icosahedron: a polyhedron with twenty faces that are equilateral triangles

irregular polygon: a two dimensional figure where all sides and all angles are not congruent

irregular prism: a prism that has a base that is an irregular polygon and the faces are not equally sized

isosceles triangle: a triangle that has at least two congruent sides

interior: the inside of an angle

interior angle: the inner angle where two sides of a polygon come together

intersecting lines: lines that meet at a point

kite: a quadrilateral with two pairs of adjacent sides that are congruent

lateral faces: any face or surface that is not a base

line: a straight path that is endless in both directions

line of symmetry: the line that divides a figure into two mirror images

line segment: a part of a line between two endpoints

measure: the number of degrees in an angle

net: a two-dimensional pattern that can be folded to make a three-dimensional figure

nonagon: a nine-sided polygon

non-collinear points: three or more points not in the same straight line

non-polyhedron: a three-dimensional figure that has curved surfaces

obtuse angle: an angle with a measure greater than 90°

Glossary (cont.)

obtuse triangle: a triangle with one obtuse angle

octagon: an eight-sided polygon

octahedron: a polyhedron with eight faces that are equilateral triangles

parallel lines: lines that never intersect

parallelogram: a quadrilateral with opposite sides parallel and opposite sides congruent

pentagon: a five-sided polygon

pentagonal prism: a prism with two pentagonal bases

pentagonal pyramid: a pyramid with a pentagonal base

perpendicular: at right angles

perpendicular lines: lines that intersect to form right angles

perimeter: the distance around a figure

pi: π; the ratio of a circle's circumference to its diameter; the approximate value is 3.14159265…

plane: an imaginary unlimited flat surface

platonic solid: an object where all the faces are identical and the same number of faces meet at each vertex

point: a single location or position

polygon: a two-dimensional, closed figure that is formed by joining three or more line segments called sides at their endpoints or vertices

polyhedron: a closed plane figure; three-dimensional figure with all flat surfaces

prism: a polyhedron with two parallel bases that are congruent polygons and faces that are parallelograms

protractor: an instrument that measures angle degrees

pyramid: a polyhedron with triangles for lateral faces (faces that are not bases) and one base

quadrilateral: a polygon with four sides and four vertices or corners

radius: the distance from the center to a point on the circle; it also may refer to the segment joining the center with a point on the circle

ray: a part of a line that extends in one direction from one endpoint

rectangle: a quadrilateral with four interior right angles; opposite sides are parallel and congruent

rectangular prism: a prism with two rectangular bases

rectangular pyramid: a pyramid with a rectangular base

reflection: one of three basic types of transformations; a reflection flips a figure over a line of symmetry

reflex angle: an angle that is greater than 180° but less than 360°

regular polygon: a two-dimensional figure where all sides and all angles are congruent

regular prism: a three-dimensional object with bases that are regular polygons and faces that are congruent

right angle: an angle that measures 90°

right triangle: a triangle with one right angle

rhombus: a parallelogram with adjacent sides congruent

rotation: one of three basic types of transformations; to turn a figure about an axis or center

scalene triangle: a triangle with no congruent sides or angles

sector: a pie-shaped portion of the area of a circle

semicircle: half a circle

sides: the arms made from two line segments, rays, or lines

similar: two-dimensional figures that have the same shape but can be different sizes

simple polygon: a closed figure with sides that do not cross over each other

skew lines: the straight lines in different planes that do not intersect and are not parallel

square: a rectangle with adjacent sides congruent; it is also a parallelogram and a quadrilateral

straight angle: an angle that measures 180°

square units: the units used to measure area

surface area: the total area of the surface of a three-dimensional object

supplementary angles: two angles whose measures total 180°

symmetry: the correspondence in size, shape, and relative position of parts on opposite sides of a dividing line or median plane or about a center

tetrahedron: a polyhedron with four faces that are equilateral triangles

three-dimensional (3-D): an object that has height, width, and depth

transformation: produces a copy, or image, of an original figure in a new position

translation: one of three basic types of transformations; a translation slides a figure from one place to another

transversal: the line that crosses two parallel lines

trapezoid: a quadrilateral with only one pair of opposite sides parallel

triangle: a polygon that has three interior angles formed by three line segments, or sides

triangular prism: a prism with two triangular bases

triangular pyramid: a pyramid with a triangular base

two-dimensional (2-D): plane figures with width and height, but no thickness

vertex: the endpoint that is shared by two rays that meet to form an angle; a corner on a polygon or solid figure (plural: vertices)

vertices: endpoints

vertical angle: an angle formed when two lines or line segments intersect

volume: the space occupied by a three-dimensional figure

Answer Keys

Unit 1

Points, Lines, and Rays (p. 3)
1. intersecting 2.   perpendicular
3. parallel 4. through 6. answers will vary.
7. parallel 8. intersecting 9. parallel
10. intersecting

Relationship Among Points, Lines, and Planes (p. 5)
1. coplanar   2. coplanar   3. collinear
4. 15   5. 21   6. 28   7. 36   8. 45
9. Formula should convey that s = the sum of the number of points plus the number of segments of the plane preceding the current plane. Ex. For D, add the points and segments for C. 4 + 6 = 10.

Identifying Angles (p. 7)
1. right   2. obtuse 3. acute   4. reflex
5. straight 6. full rotation   7. D
8. CDF or FDC 9. obtuse 10. CD and DF
11. CBD or DBE 12. CBE or ABE
13. CBA 14. DBA

The Transversal and Angles (p. 9)
1. $\overleftrightarrow{HI}$ 2. interior angles: 3, 4, 5, and 6
3. exterior angles: 1, 2, 7, and 8
4. alternate exterior angles: 1 and 8, 2 and 7
5. alternate interior angles: 3 and 6, 4 and 5
6. corresponding angles: 2 and 6, 4 and 8,
   1 and 5, 3 and 7

Measuring Angles (p. 11)
1. 10° 2. 90° 3. 10° 4. 110° 5. 60°
6. 45° 7. 16° 8. 20° 9. 35° 10. 170°
11. 45° 12. 105°   13. 120°

More About Angles (p. 13)
1. $\angle EDF$ and $\angle CDE$ 2. interior points: I
   and N, exterior points: O, U, T
3. $\angle 1$ and $\angle 2$, $\angle 1$ and $\angle 5$
4. $\angle 2$ and $\angle 3$ 5. $\angle 2$ and $\angle 5$ 6. 90°
7. $\angle 5 = 25°$, $\angle 3 = 65°$, $\angle 1 = 155°$
8. $\angle 2 = 30°$, $\angle 5 = 30°$, $\angle 1 = 150°$
9. $\angle 2 = 80°$, $\angle 5 = 80°$, $\angle 3 = 10°$

Unit 1: Assessment (p. 14)
1. c   2. c   3. c   4. c   5. d   6. c
7. d   8. a   9. c   10. b   11. b   12. b

Unit 2

Polygons (p. 17)
1. regular   2. regular   3. irregular
4. irregular   5. simple   6. complex
7. simple   8. complex   9. concave
10. convex   11. convex   12. concave

Regular and Irregular Polygons (p. 19)
1. pentagon   2. square   3. hexagon
4. octagon   5. trapezoid
6. rectangle or parallelogram 7. parallelogram
8. quadrilateral 9. regular   10. regular
11. irregular   12. irregular

Polygons Called Triangles (p. 21)
1. vertex   2. side   3.   interior angles
4. a square should indicate a right triangle
5. 90° 6. 180°   7. a square
8. capital letters   9. lower-case letters
10. congruent   11. with the same number
    of tick-marks   12. an arc 13. $\angle$

Classifying Triangles (p. 23)
1. right   2. obtuse   3. acute 4. obtuse
5. scalene 6. isosceles 7. equilateral
8. scalene 9. b   10. a

Find Unknown Interior Angle in Given Triangles (p. 25)
1. 48° 2. 55° 3. 25° 4. 40° 5. 19°
6. 30° 7. 50° 8. 102° 9. 40°   10. 50°
11. 30° 12. 50°

Polygons Called Quadrilaterals (p. 27)
1. kite   2. rectangle   3. rhombus
4. parallelogram   5. square 6. trapezoid
7. B,C,E,G   8. B,G 9. E,G   10. D,F
11. A,B,C,D,E,F,G

Find Unknown Interior Angle in Given Quadrilaterals (p. 29)
1. 360°   2. 70, 233, 233, $x = 127°$
3. 85, 255, $x = 105°$ 4. 60, 280, 280, $x = 80°$
5. $x = 55°$ 6. $x = 60°$ 7. $x = 62°$

Find Unknown Interior Angle in Given Parallelograms (p. 31)
1. sides P and S & sides Q and R
2. sides A and D & sides B and C
3. Sides F and G & sides E and H
4. 360°   5. 124°   6. 75°   7. 135°

8. $B = 130°$, $C = 50°$
9. $L = 90°$, $M = 90°$, $O = 90°$
10. $B = 43°$, $D = 137°$

Congruent or Similar? (p. 33)
1. similar   2. congruent   3. similar
4. congruent   5. similar   6. congruent
7. $\angle U$ 8. $\angle T$ 9. $\angle S$ 10. $\overline{UT}$ 11. $\overline{TS}$
12. $\overline{SU}$ 13. $\angle UST$

Lines of Symmetry (p. 35)
1. 8   2. 4   3. 5   4. 3   5. 6   6. 2
7. 1   8. 1   9. 1   10. 1
11.   12.   13.

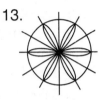

Transformations (p. 37)
1. translation   2. reflection   3. rotation
4. students draw a translation of "H"
5. students draw a translation of a rhombus
6. students draw a translation of a "6"
7. students draw a reflection of a triangle
8. students draw a reflection of a "Q"
9. students draw a reflection of an arrow
10. students draw a 90° rotation of an arrow
11. students draw a 180° rotation of a arrow
12. students draw a 270° of a pentagon

Unit 2: Assessment (p. 38)
1. d   2. b   3. d   4. a   5. c   6. c
7. b   8. a   9. d   10. d   11. d   12. a
13. a   14. c

Unit 3
Properties of Circles (p. 41)
1. D 2. $\overline{FH}$, also $\overline{CE}$, $\overline{FG}$ 3. $\overline{CE}$, $\overline{FG}$
4. $\overline{DE}$, $\overline{DG}$, $\overline{DC}$, $\overline{DF}$ 5. 360°   6. 40°
7. circumference   8. radius
9. circumference   10. diameter

Find the Radius and Diameter of a Circle (p. 43)
1. 8.6 in.   2. 18 cm   3. 5.8 cm
4. 10 cm   5. 1 m   6. 7.5 m
7. 45 m   8. 18.5 m
9. radius answers: 5.5 cm, 9 cm, 14.3 cm
   diameter answers: 14 cm, 17 cm, 26.4 cm
10. No. The lid will be too small. The diameter would only be 8 cm. 11. 27 ft. 12. 11 in.

Circumference of a Circle (p. 45)
1. 23.9 cm   2. 20.1 m   3. 12.2 mm
4. 7.5 m   5. 100.5 m   6. 42.7 cm
7. 15.1 mm   8. 50.2 m   9. 125.6 ft.
10. 25.1 ft.   11. 38.2 cm   12. 99.4 cm
13. 4,710 ft.

Area of Circles (p. 47)
1. 105.63 cm^2 2. 58.06 cm^2 3. 452.16 cm^2
4. 566.35 cm^2 5. 200.96 m^2 6. 379.94 m^2
7. 4,899.19 m^2 8. 415.27 m^2 9. 113.04 ft.^{2}
10. 7,850 ft.^{2} 11. 13,266.5 square miles
12. The 18 in. pizza gives more pizza for the money. There is more than 2 times the amount in the 18 in. for $13. It would take more than 2 12 in. pizzas; 2 would cost $14. The 18 in. pizza costs approx. $0.05 per sq. in. and the 12 in. pizza costs approx. $0.06 per sq. in.

Area of Semicircles (p. 49)
1. 25.12 m^2 2. 47.49 cm^2 3. 76.93 in.^{2}
4. 127.17 ft.^{2} 5. 113.43 cm^2 6. 273.56 m^2
7. 47.49 in.^{2} 8. 321.05 ft.^{2} 9. 226.08 in.^{2}
10. 14.13 in.^{2} 11. 1.57 m^2 12. 794.81 m^2

Unit 3: Assessment (p. 50)
1. c   2. b   3. a   4. b   5. d   6. c
7. a   8. a   9. b   10. c   11. c   12. d
13. c   14. a

Unit 4
Three-Dimensional Figures (p. 53)
1. face   2. edge   3. vertex
4. triangle   5. pentagon
6. rectangle, pentagon
7. rectangle, triangle
8. 8, 12, 6   9. 6, 10, 6
10. 0, 0, 1

Prisms (p. 55)
1. 6, 9, 5, triangle, rectangle
2. 8, 12, 6, square or rectangle, rectangle
3. 10, 15, 7, pentagon, rectangle
4. 12, 18, 8, hexagon, rectangle

Pyramids (p. 57)
1. 4, 6, 4, triangle, triangle
2. 5, 8, 5, rectangle, triangle
3. 6, 10, 6, pentagon, triangle
4. 7, 12, 7, hexagon, triangle

Circular Objects (p. 59)
1. 1, 1, 1, 1   2. 0, 2, 2, 1   3. 0, 2, 2, 1
4. 0, 0, 0, 1   5. Answers vary.
6. Answers vary.

Platonic Solids (p. 61)
1. 4, 6, 4, triangle   2. 8, 12, 6, square
3. 6, 12, 8, triangle   4. 20, 30, 12, pentagon
5. 12, 30, 20, triangle

Nets (p. 63)
1. 2, 4, square, square, cube
2. 1, 4, square, triangle, square pyramid
3. 2, 4, square, rectangle, rectangular prism
4. 1, 1, circle, semicircle, cone
5. 2, 1, circle, rectangle, cylinder

Unit 4: Assessment (p. 64)
1. b   2. c   3. d   4. d   5. a   6. b
7. c   8. c   9. b   10. a   11. d   12. c
13. d

Unit 5
Perimeter of Polygons (p. 67)
1. 21 cm   2. 50 ft.   3. 54 in.   4. 24 in.
5. 28 cm   6. 8 ft.   7. 36 in.   8. 159 in.
9. 24 in.   10. 72.52 in.   11. 24 ft.
12. 57.68 cm   13. L = 11 yds., W = 5 yds.
14. The hexagon has the greatest perimeter. It
is 42 inches. The pentagon has a perimeter
of 40 inches.

Area of Irregular Regions (p. 69)
1. 9 (6 whole squares and 6 half-squares)
2. 6$\frac{1}{2}$ (2 whole square and 9 half-squares)
3. 17$\frac{1}{2}$ (9 whole squares and 17 half-squares)
4. Answers vary.   5. Answers vary.
6. $A \approx 24$ sq. cm   7. $A \approx 16.5$ sq. cm

Area of Triangles (p. 71)
1. 6 in.^{2} 2. 36 m^2 3. 60 cm^2
4. 20 yds.^{2} 5. 24 ft.^{2} 6. 120 cm^2
7. b = 8 cm   8. h = 12 ft.

Area of a Quadrilateral (p. 73)
1. 27 ft.^{2} 2. 81 cm^2 3. 96 in.^{2} 4. 40 m^2
5. 15 cm^2 6. 84 m^2 7. 180 sq. ft.
8. 38 in.   9. 84 in.^{2} 10. 13 ft.

Area of Composite Figures (p. 75)
1. 19 cm^2 2. 75 m^2 3. 48 m^2 4. 94 ft.^{2}
5. 105.12 cm^2 6. 16.07 ft.^{2} 7. x = 12 yd.,
   y = 5 yd., P = 50 yd., A = 92 yd.^{2}
8. x = 5 in., y = 3 in., P = 46 in., A = 65 in.^{2}
9. 146.24 sq. ft.   10. 45 sq. ft.

Surface Area of Prisms (p. 77)
1. 636 cm^2 2. 944 cm^2 3. 168 cm^2
4. 640 cm^2 5. 152 cm^2 6. 314 cm^2
7. 57.5 sq. ft. (Remember, no top)
8. 2,480 sq. ft. (Remember, no floor)

Surface Area of Pyramids (p. 79)
1. 156 cm^2 2. 148.1 in.^{2} 3. 189 m^2
4. 77.5 ft.^{2} 5. 183.95 m^2
6. 236.875 m^2 7. 1,375 sq. ft. 8. 3,185 m^2

Surface Area of Cones and Cylinders (p. 81)
1. 244.92 cm^2 2. 131.88 in.^{2} 3. 593.46 cm^2
4. 301.44 cm^2 5. 376.8 m^2 6. 301.44 ft.^{2}
7. Penny's can has the larger surface area.
   Her can has 362.68 sq. in.; Liam's can has
   353.25 sq. in.
8. 2,034.72 sq. in.

Volume of Rectangular Prisms (p. 83)
1. 27 in.^{3} 2. 320 m^3 3. 864 ft.^{3}
4. 270 in.^{3} 5. 6 in.^{3} 6. 626.8 cm^3
7. 4,320 in.^{3} 8. 940.9 cm^3
9. 9,600 cu. ft.   10. 1,440 cu. ft.

Volume of Triangular Prisms (p. 85)
1. 8,580 ft.^{3} 2. 450 ft.^{3} 3. 9,568 m^3
4. 96 ft.^{3} 5. 240 cm^3 6. 69,382 mm^3
7. She should choose the triangular prism. It
   has a volume of 120.75 cu. in. The rectangular prism has a volume of 207 cu. in.

Volume of Cylinders (p. 87)
1. 100.48 m^3 2. 200.96 in.^{3} 3. 157 ft.^{3}
4. 3,140 cm^3 5. 141.3 m^3 6. 150.72 m^3
7. 35.33 cu. in. 8. 190.76 cu. ft.
9. Megan's container has the greater volume.
   It has 237.38 cu. m. Sue's container has
   107.7 cu. m.

Unit 5: Assessment (p. 88)
1. a   2. c   3. d   4. b   5. c   6. c
7. b   8. d   9. b   10. b   11. a   12. c